Burning
THE Midnight
Oil

Burning ㅌ Midnight Oil

ILLUMINATING WORDS FOR THE LONG NIGHT'S JOURNEY INTO DAY

PHIL COUSINEAU

FOREWORD BY JEFF DOWD

VIVA
EDITIONS

Published in the United States by Viva Editions, an imprint of
Cleis Press, Inc., 2246 Sixth Street, Berkeley, California 94710.

Printed in the United States.
Cover photograph: iStockphoto
Cover design: Scott Idleman/Blink
Text design: Frank Wiedemann
First Edition.
10 9 8 7 6 5 4 3 2 1

Trade paper ISBN: 978-1-936740-73-4
E-book ISBN: 978-1-936740-77-2

Library of Congress Cataloging-in-Publication Data

Burning the midnight oil : illuminating words for the long night's journey into day /
Phil Cousineau [editor].
    pages cm
  ISBN 978-1-936740-73-4 (pbk)
1. Insomnia--Literary collections. 2. Night--Literary collections. 3. Morning--Literary collections. I. Cousineau, Phil editor of compilation.
PN6071.I58B86 2014
808.8'0353--dc23
                        2013028623

Burning the midnight oil in a late-night taverna, Olympia, Greece, 2008.

To Alexander Eliot and Jane Winslow Eliot,
fellow nighthawks

Burning the Midnight Oil, Notre Dame, Paris, 1974.
Photography by Phil Cousineau

contents

"Wee spend our mid-day sweat, or mid-night oyle;
Wee tyre the night in thought; the day in toyle."

— FRANCIS QUARLES, *EMBLEMES*, 1635

"Learn to reverence night to put away the vulgar
fear of it, for, with the banishment of night from the
experience of man, there vanishes as well a religious
emotion, a poetic mood, which gives depth to the
adventure of humanity."

— HENRY BESTON

"In the light, we read the inventions of others;
in the darkness we invent our own stories…
Darkness promotes speech."

— ALBERTO MANGUEL

The Night Express to Our Soul

Since we were children, as our brains developed, we were often told, "Don't do this. Do that!" and warned, "Don't open that door!" Not that door to the mysterious, unpredictable world of our imagination—it could be dangerous and light our fire, even deadly—or, worse yet, piss off the gods and lead to Eternal Damnation.

Can it get any worse? Sure. What we would have to live with by submitting to the local Head Honcho's rules and regs: Terminal Boredom, as our minds drift toward atrophy from their natural tendency to expand and diffuse into the realm of ideas and sensations.

Rigid society's fears and lack of imagination can leave us with a garden where the only vegetables that grow are the ones they believe are good for us—and none of that tasty, intoxicating fruit that makes us imagine the unimaginable.

Fortunately for us, the highway to hell has an on-ramp nearby, every time the sun sets.

Sometime in the twilight years of the twentieth century, filmmakers Joel and Ethan Coen decided to have some fun at my expense—I'm a Big Easy target, especially when they transformed me from an activist to a slacker.

We were all fortunate to have the great actor Jeff Bridges play Jeff Lebowski, with my relaxed style and moniker—the Dude, Duder, or Duderino, if you're not into the whole brevity thing. Cut to *The Big Lebowski*. Incredibly, the movie becomes what French filmmaker François Truffaut refers to in *Close Encounters of the Third Kind* as a *"phénomène sociologique,"* with a much wider audience than a "cult classic." Surprisingly, the twisted film-noir-on-nitrous-oxide entertains across party lines and sports teams; cops and soldiers watch it as religiously as college kids and dopers. Hence, when I speak or even hang in public throughout the world, people come up to me and say:

"Hey. I just want to thank you for being my hero."

To which I respond, "Why me? You mean Jeff Bridges—the Dude in the movie?"

"No, you. The real Dude! You were the inspiration. You changed my life."

"To what? Become a slacker like the Dude? Whatever you do, don't drop out of college."

"No. To tell it like it is! Like the Dude does. He's not afraid to tell the truth. And to stay loyal to my good friends—even the ones who are assholes sometimes, like Walter."

I couldn't quite grasp this concept of the slacker as beacon of truth until I was giving a workshop with our author, Phil Cousineau, on "Myth, Magic, and Movies," in, of all places, the Huxley Room at the Esalen Institute, in Big Sur, California. So to connect my doors of perception and tie the room together, Phil surmised:

"I can't help thinking about 'the Dude' as living large in the tradition of the Holy Fool. Since ancient times it's been believed that the artist, the jester, the saint, and the fool all share the sacred function of helping us see through the illusions of the world. In our day that's the role that Charlie Chaplin, the Marx Brothers, Jon Stewart, Louis C.K., Ellen DeGeneres, Tina Fey, and Chris Rock fulfill in all their goofy glory. Jeff Dowd walks among them as an authentic holy fool pointing out the absurdities of the world with his soul on fire."

So in a world where so many of us feel we have to wear masks all day at work or in our relationships to survive, even the ramblings and protestations of the stoner Dude may help us throw off those masks and bring us back a bit to who we really are, who we really want to be, and open up the mysterious grandeur of our imagination.

This Holy Fool feels fortunate to join you and all the great artists in this book who have entered the Grand Central Station of the Mind and have passed by the très boring Orient Express on Track #1 to hop on either the Love Train (Track 69) or, in this case, the Night Express to our Soul, somewhere at the dark end of the station that leads, if perchance we survive, to the light of life—the secret source. No risk/ no reward from this nocturnal thrill ride through our subconscious.

Or we can just die a slow death of Terminal Boredom like all those Old-School Squares and Scaredy-Cats who try to lord it over us through disingenuously sharing their fears as if they were the singular reality.

Not this fella. This Dude rants and rambles:

Ride On! Write on! Sing on! Create On! Dream on through the Dark Night of the Soul.

Power to our Imagination!

Let's dream, imagine, and make our world the best of times for all!

The Dude Abides!

Jeff Dowd
Santa Monica, California

The Darkness that Heals

● ◐ ○ ○ ○ ◑ ●

"Night time is the right time,
to be with the one you love."

— RAY CHARLES

The mammoth steel presses bellowed, the praying mantis-like stamping machines screeched. Forklifts hummed across the factory floor carrying pallets of coiled steel wire. The midnight coal train clacketed down the railroad tracks behind the factory on its way to the River Rouge Plant, in the burning bowels of Detroit. The moment the whistle blew to signal the end of my ten-hour night shift at the steel factory, I hustled over to the time clock. Quickly, I punched my time card and slipped it back into the long metal card rack on the wall. As I turned to leave, I noticed some newly scrawled graffiti on the cement block wall:

"It takes all day to get up
and all night to get down."

To this day I don't know who wrote those pugnacious words, but I've never forgotten them. I still marvel over how well they captured our defiant factory-rat spirit during the four benighted years I spent at Industrial & Automotive Fasteners in Detroit. Hardly a day went by without someone groaning about how tough it was to *get up* every day for work. Then again, hardly a night went by—especially when the weekends rolled around—without hearing somebody boast about how they were going to *get down* as soon as they got off work. The street jive insinuated a night of hard drinking, heavy gambling, skirt chasing, or drag racing down Woodward Avenue. But it was more than braggadocio. It was a riff on "Night Time Is the Right Time," the Ray Charles song that was playing on the radio in those years because whatever happened after midnight was *our* time. If we could "get up," we could get to work on time; but if we could "get down," we might get to that place beyond time that exists in the shadows of the night.

"Somewhere," said Schick, the night shift foreman, "the real life is waiting for us."

For the handful of us who were working our way through college, *getting down* meant pulling all-nighters in the hope we might catch up with whatever courses we'd fallen behind in during the week. After slaving away through those long night shifts and then doing homework until three or four in the morning I had to ratchet my weary bones to get up out of bed. For me, the sound of an alarm clock going off, especially during the dark dawns of winter, was like an ice pick in my ear. So I was rarely on time for my eight a.m. journalism class twenty miles away, at the University of Detroit.

One miserable morning during my senior year, my professor Judy Serrin noticed my bleary-eyed expression as, an embarrassing twenty minutes late, I slunk in. It may have been the oil stains on my hands or the smell of factory phosphate on my clothes, but a look of concern crossed her face as I passed by her desk. "It looks like you've been burning the midnight oil," she whispered. Then with unexpected compassion, she added softly, "Hand in your stories whenever you can."

It was very Detroit of her to say so.

Burning the midnight oil. My grandparents had used the expression to describe how late they were forced to work, night after night, in the family pharmacy, during the stark years of the Depression. Roger Turner, my first newspaper editor, at the *Wayne Dispatch*, had employed the phrase as a warning when he hired me to work the graveyard shift. But there was something else, something shiver-inducing in my professor's voice.

Rust Belt respect is what it was.

In those years, in those factories and shops, people took pride in how hard and long they worked. You worked at whatever task you were engaged in—churning out steel nuts for the car companies or churning out essays in college—until you were done, even if you had to burn the midnight oil.

No excuses, no whining, no cheating.

"Cold fact," sang Sixto Rodriquez, the legendary Detroit songwriter, who was working night shifts a mile away, down at Dodge Main, my last year in the factory, then playing the blues clubs down along the Detroit River. "Just a cold fact." It was a given. If you were going to do anything worthwhile in your life, you had to burn the midnight oil.

Until the early seventeenth-century the word for working late into the night was *elucubrate*, which was defined in 1623, by Henry Cockeram in *The English Dictionarie, or, An Interpreter of Hard English Words*, "to doe a thing by candlelight." Twelve years later, in 1635, the English novelist and poet Francis Quarles wrote a poem called *Emblemes*, which featured the first published reference to another way to elongate our days:

> *"Wee spend our mid-day sweat,*
> *or mid-night oyle;*
> *Wee tyre the night in thought,*
> *the day in toyle."*

We tire the night in thought; the day in toil.

In other words, it takes all day to get up, all night to get down.

The poet's archaic but comprehensible language opens a window onto the seventeenth century, when the invention of street lamps and longer-burning lights in the home liberated people from the tyranny of darkness.

Originally referring to the actual act of burning oil in lamps for light and safety, the expression "burning the midnight oil" has come to mean any practice that allows us to stay up later, see better, push the natural rhythms, work overtime, even unravel the mysteries of the impenetrable darkness. Ever since I have equated it with working late, working hard, working it, as in working the system, using every ounce of strength and wit to get through life. To do that, I believe, you have to burn the midnight oil.

Years ago, while researching the history of cafés, I came across a poster for the Faggs Coffee House, established in Wellington, New Zealand, in 1926:

> *Any time is coffee time*
> *When burning the midnight oil,*
> *Whatever your brand of toil—*
> *The swot, the poem, the woo—*
> *Our coffee will see you through.*

Together, the invention of longer-burning lamps and the concoction of coffee made for a revolution in the way people regarded the night. For centuries, life after dark had been dreaded and even avoided by sleeping and waking early. The night was dangerous; the night was cruel. It was the absence of day and light, not a value in itself. Night time demanded respect and even avoidance, usually by way of sleep.

Over time, the way people experienced the dark was transformed alongside a newfound belief in the strange beauty of after-dark, which was captured by the chiaroscuro of Rembrandt the shadow-strewn world of *The Maltese Falcon*, or the radiant photographs of distant galaxies coming back from the Hubble Space Telescope. Although known mostly for his playful novels, like *Alice in Wonderland* and *The Hunting of the Snark*, Lewis Carroll was also an inventor. His most noteworthy device was the "nyctograph," which he fondly described as an "indelible memorandum book" that allowed him the freedom of not getting out of bed, as he put it, "at 2 a.m. on a winter night to light a candle." The book was really a wooden board that featured alternating square and round holes, which he used to mark the letters of the alphabet with a pen or stylus. In absolute darkness he was able to record "some happy thoughts which would probably be otherwise forgotten." This depth of devotion to the night world goes a long to help explain the uncanny way Carroll was able to take a form of dictation, as it were, straight from his phantasmagorical imagination.

Recently, I found myself at the venerable Hodges Figgis Bookstore on Dawson Street, in Dublin, searching for an obscure book on one of my favorite, if arcane, topics—the bardic training schools of medieval Ireland. I've long been mystified as to how it was possible for Ireland's revered Celtic poets to memorize such a staggering amount of poetry, myths, curses, and riddles that it was commonly believed among peasants and kings alike that they possessed magical powers.

As if welcoming the challenge, the bookseller found the volume I'd been searching for for years, *Irish Bardic Poetry*, by Osborn Bergin, first published in 1912. His learned introduction included an obscure passage from an antiquarian book, published in 1703, by the doubly named Martin Martin, who wrote in his travelogue, *Descriptions of the Western Islands of Scotland*, about the "Dark Cells" where Scottish bards studied in their very singular way: "They shut their Doors and Windows for a Days time, and lie on their backs with a Stone upon their Belly, and Plads [plaids] about their Heads, and their Eyes being covere'd they pump their Brains for Rhetorical Encomium or Panegyrick."

Apparently, there is a light that we can find only in the dark, which is the very definition of the inspiration that brings about new thoughts and ideas.

The French painter Henri Matisse needed only four one-syllable words to describe this ineffable power, "Black is a force."

I've been haunted by the night since I was a young boy growing up in Wayne, a small town outside Detroit, ominously named for Mad Anthony Wayne, the Civil War hero. Listening to Ernie Harwell's late-night broadcasts of Tigers baseball games on my transistor radio, canoeing and camping under the stars on Isle Royale, lazing in the grass underneath a shower of fireworks along the Detroit River, attending midnight mass at Wayne St. Mary's, or, crazy as it sounds now, driving all night in my Uncle Cy's 1965 Hot Rod Lincoln up to the Mackinaw Bridge with my high school friends. Just for the thrill of watching the sun rise over Lake Superior....

Looking back, it's as if I was in training for a life of noctivagating the world: night walks around the cobbled streets of the Latin Quarter in Paris; night writing on Naxos with Greek fishermen; riding a train all night from Oslo to Narvik, in the Arctic Circle, to witness the aurora borealis; tracking elephants at night to a watering hole in Namibia.

Looking back over my shoulder at the unreeling film of my life, it seems I have always felt more at home in the night world than in the day world, more comfortable with nighthawks than early birds.

This anthology reflects my fascination with "eating the darkness," as a shaman in the Philippines described to me the act of storytelling by firelight. For years I have been gathering strange material for my Odditorium, which celebrates life after dark, from quotes, poems, chants, and song lyrics to short stories and novels, and even a night-game box score about the oddly luminous aspects of night time.

The result closely resembles what used to be called a *noctuary*, a record or journal of nocturnal contemplations that aspires to be a source of inspiration for the nighthawk brooding in an all-night diner, an insomniacs guide to the dark night of the soul, or a beguiling companion book to sit alongside a warm brandy on the bed stand.

We now live in a 24/7 world where lights blaze everywhere, as any astronaut can tell you, and darkness is harder and harder to find, as any astronomer can verify. If we are to survive this onslaught of light and withstand the pressure to be always working, then we will have to work on what my main man, Detroit's own Bob Seger, called our "night moves."

Burning the Midnight Oil is offered in the spirit of one of my boyhood heroes, Mark Twain, whose daughters insisted that their father regale them with a different story every night before they went to bed. They would name different objects in the house and insist that he use them in his nocturnal tales, whose purpose was to entertain, of course, but also to become, as Robert Frost suggests in his totemic poem, more acquainted with the coming dark.

I imagine this collection to serve a similar function, an offer to the reader of a wide range of stories, poems, chants, and song lyrics designed to celebrate the dark side of the moon, our endarkenment rather than our enlightenment.

Consider the marvel. One day I was being interviewed at one of the movie studios in Hollywood when I noticed a curious sign on the door of a room where special effects were being created:

Don't open the door.
The darkness may leak out.

I am haunted by the night.

Phil Cousineau
North Beach, San Francisco
June 2013

PART I:

THE TWILIGHT ZONE

"There is nothing in the dark that isn't there when the lights are on."

— ROD SERLING

S wiftly, night comes on. Dusk is upon us. Darkness rushes in. The crepuscular voices in this opening section remind us that night is more than earth's dark turn away from the sun. It is the first step in the long journey into the original twilight zone, the liminal world between night and day that has haunted human beings since the red dawn of time. Through the soulful picture language of mythology, the Greek poet Hesiod tells us why. Out of the Chaos at the moment of creation, he writes in *The Theogony*, came the first gods, the personification of the powers of the world. One was Eros, god of love and desire; another was Erebus, the face of darkness, and also Nyx, goddess of the night. The numinous imagery tells us that night was born of desire, which the Greeks believed to be one of the great forces of nature, and darkness. It is the love of darkness—soul work—and night brings forth light and day, but not for the usual reasons.

"Last night / the rain / spoke to me," writes Mary Oliver, "slowly saying / what joy / to come falling / out of the brisk cloud / to be happy again." This world of fog and shadows, which we are exploring here, alternates between loneliness and exultation, yearning and the white-stripe fever of driving in the dark. What the contributors here share in common is an embrace of *endarkenment*.

Usually regarded as a poet of crystalline light and clarity, Sappho captures the often lacerating loneliness of sleeping alone while granting it dignity. The Indian polymath Rabindranath Tagore offers a short poem about nature's own lamps, in "Fireflies." The bard of New Hampshire, Robert Frost, calls for us to befriend or become "acquainted" with the night, while Emily Dickinson offers an astonishing insight, that the night is vital because "Either the Darkness alters— / Or something in the sight / Adjusts itself to Midnight..." The transcendent nature writer and novelist Annie Dillard describes how the very stars "trembled and stirred" with her breath. The English novelist and poet Thomas Hardy hauntingly evokes the central theme of this opening section, in "Afterwards," where he writes that night is full of mysteries and a poet is one of whom it is said, "He was a man who used to notice such things." The labyrinthine Argentinean Jorge Luis Borges has a vision in "Baruch Spinoza" of the medieval philosopher "building God in the twilight." Irish novelist and musicologist P.J. Curtis encounters an old traveling man who describes "the book of the night sky, every night a different page." The Milwaukee poet Antler sees the stars as the beautiful breasts of a cosmic mother. Poet and novelist Linda Watanabe McFerrin explores a different kind of ecstasy in "A Little Night Music." Her sentences are an exercise in heavy breathing: "Later, his arms still around me, we sat for a while, like nesting boxes, braced against nightfall, looking out toward the shadowed horizon." She captures not only the elusive frisson of freedom at night, but also the way that romance can act as a bulwark against the loneliness of the long-distance traveler who is alone at night.

Not only desire but fear is aroused by the fall of light, as we learn in historian Huston Smith's dramatic telling of his terror of lions on the Serengeti Plains as darkness began to fall.

Writer and teacher Jane Winslow Eliot tells about following in the footsteps of her grandmother, straight to the edge of the Grand Canyon, on her honeymoon.

"There had been a rhythm of the day and now there was a rhythm of the night," wrote the Irish poet Padraic Colum. Nightfall can accompany astronomers, lovers, and comedians alike, as we learned from George Carlin: "Tonight's forecast: dark. Continued dark tonight turning to partly light in the morning."

The question of the dark mysteries hovers, so it is helpful to learn what the *noctivagators*, the night walkers, have to say about their own encounters with the world of tumbling light, the twilight, just before dark.

Clearly, there are light and dark secrets. The night moves on, revealing stars and sleep and the darkness that restores.

"This will do," Annie Dillard thought. "This will do."

It will, it will.

BUT I SLEEP ALONE

The moon is set. And the Pleiades.
It's the middle of the night.
Time passes.
But I sleep alone.

SAPPHO, GREEK POET, 625-570 B.C.E.
TRANSLATED FROM THE GREEK BY WILLIS BARNSTONE

EVENING STAR

Hesperos, you bring home all the bright dawn
scattered,
bring home the sheep,
bring home the goat, bring the child home
to her mother.

SAPPHO, GREEK POET, 625-570 B.C.E.
TRANSLATED FROM THE GREEK BY WILLIS BARNSTONE

FIREFLIES

My fancies are fireflies—
Specks of living light
twinkling in the dark.

"Let me light my lamp,"
says the star,
"And never debate
if it will help to remove the darkness."

RABINDRANATH TAGORE,
INDIAN POET AND PHILOSOPHER, 1861–1941
TRANSLATED FROM THE BENGALI BY THE AUTHOR

ACQUAINTED WITH THE NIGHT

I have been one acquainted with the night.
I have walked out in rain—and back in rain.
I have outwalked the furthest city light.

I have looked down the saddest city lane.
I have passed by the watchman on his beat

And dropped my eyes, unwilling to explain.

I have stood still and stopped the sound of feet
When far away an interrupted cry
Came over houses from another street,

But not to call me back or say good-bye;
And further still at an unearthly height,
A luminary clock against the sky

Proclaimed the time was neither wrong nor right.
I have been one acquainted with the night.

ROBERT FROST, AMERICAN POET, 1874–1963

WE GROW ACCUSTOMED TO THE DARK

We grow accustomed to the Dark—
When light is put away—
As when the Neighbor holds the Lamp
To witness her Goodbye—

A Moment—We uncertain step
For newness of the night—
Then—fit our Vision to the Dark—
And meet the Road—erect—

And so of larger—Darkness—
Those Evenings of the Brain—
When not a Moon disclose a sign—
Or Star—come out—within—

The Bravest—grope a little—
And sometimes hit a Tree
Directly in the Forehead—
But as they learn to see—

Either the Darkness alters—
Or something in the sight
Adjusts itself to Midnight—
And Life steps almost straight.

EMILY DICKINSON, AMERICAN POET, 1830–1886

Last night
the rain
spoke to me
slowly, saying,

what joy
to come falling
out of the brisk cloud,
to be happy again

in a new way
on the earth!
That's what it said
as it dropped,

smelling of iron,
and vanished
like a dream of the ocean
into the branches

and the grass below.
Then it was over.

The sky cleared.
I was standing

under a tree.
The tree was a tree
with happy leaves,
and I was myself,

and there were stars in the sky
that were also themselves
at the moment
at which moment

my right hand
was holding my left hand
which was holding the tree
which was filled with stars

and the soft rain—
imagine! imagine!
the long and wondrous journeys
still to be ours.

MARY OLIVER, AMERICAN POET AND ESSAYIST

AFTERWARDS

When the Present has latched its postern behind my tremulous stay,
And the May month flaps its glad green leaves like wings,
Delicate-filmed as new-spun silk, will my neighbors say,
"He was a man who used to notice such things"?

If it be in the dusk when, like an eyelid's soundless blink,
The dewfall-hawk comes crossing the shades to alight
Upon the wind-warped upland thorn, a gazer may thunk
"To him this must have been a familiar sight."

If I pass during some nocturnal blackness, mothy and warm,
When the hedgehog travels furtively over the lawn,
One may say, "He strove that such innocent creatures should
come to no harm,
But he could do little for them; and now he is gone."

If, when hearing that I have been stilled at last, they stand at
the door,
Watching the full-starred heavens that winter sees,
Will this thought rise on those who will meet my face no more,
"He was one who had an eye for such mysteries"?

And will any say when my bell of quittance is heard in the gloom,

And a crossing breeze cuts a pause in its outrollings,
Till they rise again, as they were a new hell's boom,
"He hears it not now, but used to notice such things"?

THOMAS HARDY,
ENGLISH NOVELIST AND POET, 1840–1928

BARUCH SPINOZA

A haze of gold, the Occident lights up
The window. Now, the assiduous manuscript
Is waiting, weighed down with the infinite.
Someone is building God in a dark cup.
A man engenders God. He is a Jew.
With saddened eyes and lemon-colored skin;
Time carries him the way a leaf, dropped in
A river, is borne off by waters to
Its end. No matter. The magician moved
Carves out his God with fine geometry;
From his disease, from nothing, he's begun
To construct God, using the word. No one
Is granted such prodigious love as he:
The love that has no hope of being loved.

JORGE LUIS BORGES,
ARGENTINE POET, NOVELIST, LIBRARIAN, 1899–1986
TRANSLATED FROM THE SPANISH BY WILLIS BARNSTONE

Like any out-of-the-way place, the Napo River in the Ecuadorian jungle seems real enough when you are there, even central. Out of the way of *what*? I was sitting on a stump at the edge of a bankside palm-thatch village, in the middle of the night, on the headwaters of the Amazon. Out of the way of human life, tenderness, or the glance of heaven?

A nightjar in deep-leaved shadow called three long notes, and hushed. The men with me talked softly in clumps: three North Americans, four Ecuadorians who were showing us the jungle. We were holding cool drinks and idly watching a hand-sized tarantula seize moths that came to the lone bulb on the generator shed beside us.

It was February, the middle of summer. Green fireflies spattered lights across the air and illumined for seconds—now here, now there— the pale trunks of enormous, solitary trees. Beneath us the brown Napo River was rising, in all silence; it coiled up the sandy bank and tangled its foam in vines that trailed from the forest and roots that looped the shore.

Each breath of night smelled sweet, more moistened and sweet than any kitchen, or garden, or cradle. Each star in Orion seemed to tremble and stir with my breath. All at once, in the thatch house across the clearing behind us, one of the village's Jesuit priests began playing an alto recorder, playing a wordless song, lyric, in a minor key, that twined over the village clearing, that caught in the big trees' canopies, muted our talk on the bankside, and wandered over the river, dissolving downstream.

This will do, I thought. This will do, for a weekend, or a season, or a home.

ANNIE DILLARD, AMERICAN WRITER

THE TIMES ARE NIGHTFALL

The times are nightfall, look, their light grows less;
The times are winter, watch, a world undone:
They waste, they wither worse; they as they run
Or bring more or more blazon man's distress.
And I not help. Nor word now of success:
All is from wreck, here, there, to rescue one—
Work which to see scarce so much as begun
Makes welcome death, does dear forgetfulness.

Or what is else? There is your world within.
There rid the dragons, root out there the sin.
Your will is law in that small commonweal....

GERARD MANLEY HOPKINS,
ENGLISH THEOLOGIAN AND POET, 1844–1889

In the Great Night

In the great night to my heart will out,
Toward me the darkness comes rattling.
In the great heart my heart will go out.

In the Blue Night

How shall I begin my song
In the blue night that is settling?
I will sit here and begin my song.

In the Dark I Enter

I can not make out what I see.
In the dark I enter.
I can not make out what I see.

Owl Woman (Juana Maxwell),
Papago healer, 1880?–1847
Translated from the Papago by Frances Densmore

BLUE MOSQUE REVERIE

A white crescent moon passes behind the long Sultan Ahmet mosque, suddenly glazing ancient Istanbul with silver light. The medieval stone archway's bowered garden frames the six needle-shaped minarets, twenty-four smaller domes like a bold border in an illuminated manuscript.

In and out of the god-source dark night fly great white streaks of seagulls, as if retracing the arabesque patterns on the mosque. Near the jasmine-scented garden walls, a peacock cries like a sleepless baby—a cry, the ancient Sufis believed, for the soul to dance. From the cafés in the labyrinthine lanes of the old city echoes the sound of slapping dominoes and haunting Turkish folk songs that crackle on old radios. In that deep pool of listening, I heard the dark consonants of long-forgotten tongues and the sultan's scraping prayers on old cobblestones wet with rain.

It was long ago that this would happen again.

PHIL COUSINEAU
ISTANBUL, TURKEY, 1992

NIGHT AND SLEEP

At the time of night-prayer, as the sun slides down,
the route the senses walk on closes, the route to be invisible
opens.

The angel of sleep then gathers and drives along the spirits;
just as the mountain keeper gathers his sheep on a slope.

And what amazing sights he offers to the descending sheep!
Cities with sparkling streets, hyacinth gardens, emerald pastures!

The spirit sees astounding beings, turtles turned to men,
men turned to angels, when sleep erases the banal.

I think one could say the spirit goes back to its old home:
it no longer remembers where it lives. And loses its fatigue.

It carries around in life so many griefs and loads
and trembles under their weight; they are gone, it is all well.

MEVLANA RUMI,
PERSIAN POET AND MYSTIC, 1207–1273
TRANSLATED FROM THE PERSIAN BY
COLEMAN BARKS AND ROBERT BLY

A HYMN TO THE NIGHT

Once, when I poured out bitter tears, when I dissolved in pain and scattered, and I was standing alone at the barren hill which hid the shape of my life in its narrow dark space—alone, as no one could be more alone, driven by unspeakable anxiety—strengthless, with just one thought left of need. As I looked around for help, could not move forwards and not backwards, and hung onto the fleeting, extinguished life with infinite craving:—then came from blue distances—from the heights of my old blessedness, a twilight shiver—and with one stroke my birth's bond ripped—Light's chains. There the earthy splendor fled and my sadness with it—misery flowed into a new, unplumbed world—You, Night-inspiration, heaven's sleep, came over me—the region lifted gently up, over the region my released and newborn spirit floated. The hill became a cloud of dust—through the cloud I saw the transfigured features of my beloved. In her eyes rested the forever—I took her hands, and my tears were a glittering and unrippable bond. Years by the thousands flew off to the distance, like storms. In her embrace I wept overjoyed tears at the new life.—It was the first and the only dream—and only since then I've felt an unchangeable, eternal faith in the heaven of Night and its Light, the beloved.

NOVALIS, GERMAN POET, 1772–1801
TRANSLATED FROM THE GERMAN BY DICK HIGGINS

> Memory is not what we remember
> but that which remembers us.
> Memory is a present that never stops passing.

> — OCTAVIO PAZ

I'm at the age when memory begins to fail me. I've always prided myself on having a sharp memory; being instantly able to recall—with total clarity, down to the smallest details—names, faces, events. Indeed I once had the ability to recall any event or scene from all the days and decades of my past.

Memory, it seems to me, lives by its own separate and immutable rules. Often, the sweetest—though sometimes more painful—recollections are triggered by a simple casual word, a familiar sound, and sometimes even a particular taste or scent.

On one particular evening in late autumn, it is a combination of such things—a distant dog barking in the frosty night air, the sweet wafting aroma of a hazel-wood fire from a nearby chimney, and the sharp, cold twinkling of a solitary star in the northern sky. Sitting alone in my kitchen, with the clock ticking off the minutes, I have the urge to breathe in the bracing autumn night air. I step outside and look skyward. Suddenly, without warning, I am propelled back down the time-tunnel of memory.

In the turn of that moment, it is the early 1950s. I am once again ten years old, it is a clear frosty night, and I am sitting by the campfire of old Rory Dubh, "Black Rory" the Traveler, the Last Prince of Thormond.

One sharp, frosty November evening as darkness fell, I pass close to the site where Rory Dubh traditionally made his camp for the night. From a distance, the perfume of his hazel-wood fire wafts gently on the still air. The yellow glow from his campfire looks like a fallen star.

In the half-light, he recognizes me and calls out for me to join him.

I approach the camp with caution. I was, I had to admit, very much in awe of this ragged old traveling man, this prince of his tribe—maybe a king even!—who now summoned me to his campfire-court. He motions me to take a seat, pointing at an up-turned butter-box by the fire while he sits, a clay-pipe protruding from his remaining uneven teeth, between the shafts of his cart.

His dark, hooded eyes never leave me as I slowly and nervously move within the circle of dancing amber firelight and settle myself on the upturned box.

Rory Dubh smiles a slow smile as I accept from him a tin mug of hot, sweet tea, which he pours from the billycan boiling on the glowing-red embers. He has many questions, all of which I shyly try to answer. What age was I now? Did I like school? Did I read books?

"Books are better for you than bread," Rory Dubh says, puffing hard at his clay-pipe and stirring the fire with his blackthorn stick.

After a long silence, he points his stick upwards and prods the dark night air above his head.

"There's my book," he says softly. "The book of the sky."

My eyes follow the stick from the glowing embers to the glowing star-spangled heavens spread above us.

"Every night, a different page. Every page, a different story to tell."

Together, in silence, we gaze deep into the frosty night air.

"Do you know anything at all about stars?" He turns to me, his eyes as bright as the hazel-stick embers. I shake my head and continue to gaze up at the carpet of diamond-hard stars twinkling overhead.

"There's the Great Bear...there's the Plow...there's the Seven Sisters, surrounded by their clans...and there's the North Star...the traveler's friend...but there"—he sweeps his arm in a wide arc—"is the Milky way...the mighty Milky Way!"

My eyes follow the wide sweep of his arm.

"Do you know what it's made up of?" he asks.

I shake my head again.

"Souls," he says softly. "The souls of the dead."

His words chill me to the bone and seem to send a shiver through the arc of stars like a soft wind stirring wind chimes in the distance.

His dreamy voice sounds far away as he continues.

"When we die, our souls fly up there to join all those who have gone before us and get in line to enter Heaven. Every star you see is a soul waiting its turn to go through the Gates of Paradise."

I stare at the great trail of shimmering light across the canopy of the heavens and try to imagine how many millions of souls went to make up this vast highway in the night sky.

"Every time we see a star fall to earth, it's another soul allowed into heaven." Rory Dubh speaks so softly now his voice is but a brittle whisper, and I know he speaks now only to himself.

"We're all heading for a place on that road of souls. All my own people are gone on ahead and they're up there now, waiting for me to join them." His old eyes scan the flight of stars as they tumble and fall towards the horizon.

"I'll be there a lot sooner than you, young fella!" He jabs his stick at me across the blazing sticks and twigs. He looks upwards again and adds, "And the better we are on this journey here below, the brighter our souls will glow on that journey above."

Rory Dubh grins a rotten-tooth grin and adds. "I'm sure you'll make a grand bright star...but not for a good long time yet with the help of the Man above!"

We sit and sip the sweet tea and lapse into silent communion. The night has deepened, and fire now casts dancing shadows on the nearby stones and whitethorn bushes, and its sparks seem to jump directly into the Milky Way to join that shining throng on their eternal journey.

Rory Dubh turns his face again toward the sky, and for a long while I watch the glow of the firelight highlight the years etched on his old, weatherworn features. When he looks at me again across the campfire I see now in his eyes—a moment ago reflecting the twinkling of distant stars—the glistening of a tear.

"Every journey we make on this old earth is but in preparation for the longer journey which awaits us all. We're all on our own separate journeys...prince or priest or pauper...each on his own road...and there is no road without bends. Never forget that, lad!"

As I slowly walk away from the circle of light and heat, my imagination races, my head now full of sky and stars. A cold November moon has risen in the east and sits for a moment on the far horizon while its pale light turns the hazel and whitethorn trees to spirits and ghosts and the stones to silver and gold. There is magic all about me now in the night air and I breathe deeply of it.

Later that same night, warm and secure by my own fireside, my thoughts fill with Rory Dubh and I long to be back with him at his campfire, peering deep into that starry road of souls.

I arise early next morning and return to his campsite in the hope to see him again but Rory Dubh the Traveller, along with Jenny, his pony, and his two dogs, had moved on.

How different things look to me in the cold morning light. The campsite now looks strangely forlorn and abandoned. The only sign of Rory Dubh's overnight stay are the ruts cut into the frosted earth by his cart-wheels, and all that remains of the magic and majesty of his royal court of the previous night are a few still-smoldering embers among the cold ash within the fire's stone circle.

I never saw Rory Dubh alive again.

Time passed, and there was no further word on Rory Dubh or his whereabouts. Then came a day in the spring of the following year that we got the news that Rory Dubh the Traveler—last Prince of Thormond—was dead. He had been found underneath his cart one freezing January morning, his frost-covered earthly remains being watched over and waked by his trusty old pony and faithful dogs. They said his wake and funeral were attended by hundreds of travelers from three counties, and he was at last laid to rest in an unmarked pauper's grave in an ancient graveyard near the road so he could hear the traveler's cart and caravans go by when spring and autumn came again.

That night I went outside to catch a glimpse of the Milky Way and whisper a prayer for the soul of Rory Dubh O'Brien—that gentle road-side emperor and descendant of kings.

My memory is not as sharp as it once was, but tonight—as I catch the pungent aroma of a hazel-wood fire, hear a dog baying somewhere in the distance—I look skyward at that splash of light painted across the moonless night sky, and I shed a tear for both myself and for that gentle, noble "man of the road," Rory Dubh the Traveler.

I fancy now I see his Star light up the Milky Way. It twinkles brighter than all the rest as he makes camp, reunited at last with his own people on his final journey along that endless Road of Souls. The long years that have separated him and me grow heavy on my shoulders, and it probably won't be too long before I set off down that same starry road on my own last journey. How I long to sit again with Rory Dubh, to warm my hands by his campfire and watch it cast long shadows which dance across the universe; to drink again his sweet tea; to gaze again into his wise old eyes and outward into space, to other lights and distant stars...and remember.

P.J. CURTIS, IRISH AUTHOR AND MUSICOLOGIST

LAST NIGHT ON SANTORINI

The sea is black. The sky is black.
The volcano is blackest of all.
The lights of the thin white town—
A scarf along the dark hard cliffs—
Tinkle their reflections on the wavelets below.
The lights of the stars cast like jewels of sand
Speckle and dimple the darkness above.
The volcano's lava is deep and porous.
It reflects nothing. It swallows all.

I stand at my tiny wooden frame window
Between soft blue curtains as sheer as shrouds.
I stare at these powers that dwarf me.
To the sea I played in afternoon sun
I am weaker than driftwood, softer than coral.
To the cliffs I climbed on an ass's back
I am equally a slave and less brazen than his bells.
To the volcano whose boulders revealed me a pebble
I am as fragile as the goat bones bleached in its crevice.
I stand by my window knowing I am nothing.
All I have is this knowing, this yearning, this seeing
That makes me love them though they swallow me whole,
That makes me salute though they do not salute back,

That makes me gambol and gamble until the time
When I am nothing but knucklebones tossed by these tides,
My fate read by the winds and the waves
Until devoured by these fires that do not die.

EDWARD TICK, AMERICAN PSYCHOTHERAPIST AND POET

THE TYGER

Tyger! Tyger! burning bright
In the forests of the night,
What immortal hand or eye
Could frame thy fearful symmetry?

In what distant deeps or skies
Burned the fire of thine eyes?
On what wings dare he aspire?
What the hand dare seize the fire?

And what shoulder, and what art,
Could twist the sinews of thy heart?
And when thy heart began to beat,
What dread hand? And what dread feet?

What the hammer? What the chain?
In what furnace was thy brain?
What the anvil? What dread grasp
Dare its deadly terrors clasp?

When the stars threw down their spears,
And watered heaven with their tears,
Did he smile his work to see?

Did he who made the Lamb make thee?

Tyger! Tyger! Burning bright
In the forests of the night,
What immortal hand or eye
Dare frame thy fearful symmetry?

WILLIAM BLAKE, ENGLISH POET AND PAINTER, 1757–1827

alone
tonight
in this house,
alone with
6 cats
who tell me
without
effort
all that there
is
to know

CHARLES BUKOWSKI,
AMERICAN POET AND NOVELIST, 1920–1994

MOTHER NURSING MILKY WAY

Mother, take me outdoors at night
   the night after I'm born
And show me the Milky Way
   with no city lights in sight,
Before I learn how to walk or talk
   when the only food I eat
      comes from your beautiful breasts,
Take me out under the stars
   to drink in their milk
      as I drink in yours,
Take me, take me out naked under the stars,
Offer me up naked to the stars,
And then let me suck milk from your breasts
   looking up at your face and infinite Milky Ways,
Yes, take me out under the stars
   before I know what stars are
      or planets or moons or comets or galaxies
   or how a man and woman make love
      to create a baby,
   before I learn how to walk or talk,
Take me dear Mother under the stars.

ANTLER, AMERICAN POET

On the rough wet grass of the back yard my father and mother have spread quilts. We all lie there, my mother, my father, my uncle, my aunt, and I too am lying there. First we were sitting up, then one of us lay down, and then we all lay down, on our stomachs, or on our sides, or on our backs, and they have kept on talking. They are not talking much, and the talk is quiet, of nothing in particular, of nothing at all in particular, of nothing at all. The stars are wide and alive, they seem each like a smile of great sweetness, and they seem very near. All my people are larger bodies than mine, quiet, with voices gentle and meaningless like the voices of sleeping birds. One is an artist, he is living at home. One is a musician, she is living at home. One is my mother who is good to me. One is my father who is good to me. By some chance, here they are, all on this earth; and who shall ever tell the sorrow of being on this earth, lying, on quilts, on the grass, in a summer evening, among the sounds of the night. May God bless my people, my uncle, my aunt, my mother, my good father, oh, remember them kindly in their time of trouble; and in the hour of their taking away.

After a little I am taken in and put to bed. Sleep, soft smiling, draws me unto her: and those receive me, who quietly treat me, as one familiar and well-beloved in that home: but will not, oh, will not, not now, not ever; but will not ever tell me who I am.

JAMES AGEE,
AMERICAN WRITER, PLAYWRIGHT AND MOVIE CRITIC, 1909–1955

At Olduvai Gorge, in South Africa, I was told that if I walked two miles from my broken down car to the nearest highway at twilight, "You *must* be eaten by lions."

Those words sounded to me like a command. They came toward the close of the day in which I *would* have been eaten by lions in the Serengeti Plain, if I had not been rescued by twelve robust Masai warriors.

Here is the story.

To attend a conference in the late 1960s, I had flown to Dar es Salam, the Haven of Peace, the capital of Tanzania. The city abuts the Serengeti Plains. Anticipating an adventure, encountering Big Game in their natural habitat, I did a bit of research. I learned that this plain is the sanctuary of the Masai tribe and that it harbors more wild game than any comparable stretch of territory in all of East Africa. The plain may seem empty, but actually it swarms with as much life as the waters of tropical seas do. It is webbed with the paths of wildebeests and gazelles, and its hollows and valleys are trampled by thousands of zebras. Buffalo invade the pastures, and occasionally the droll shape of a rhinoceros can be seen plodding across the horizon like a boulder that has come to life and is stalking its own form of adventure.

Learning this, I knew I couldn't leave the country without a glimpse of some of these animals. There were no tours in those days, but I found a fly-by-night rental car agency that had a rickety Renault that was so far gone they were desperate to get it off their lot. They sold it to me for the price of a rental.

So, as the sudden owner of a Tanzanian car, really a jalopy, I set out for the Serengeti. There were no road maps in the car, which figured, because there were no roads. Eventually, I did encounter one road sign, which I couldn't read, and in any case it had fallen over, which meant I couldn't even tell which way its arrows were meant to point.

As far as the eye could see, there was nothing except grass, rocks, and a few animals and trees.

If that wasn't ominous enough, I was scarcely into the plain when I had a flat tire and was forced to get out of the car to change it, which was not the safest or sanest thing to do in that part of the world. While I was busy cranking the car up with the tire jack, a curious giraffe ambled over and leaned across my shoulder. A little farther into the desert the car's motor sputtered and with a little gasp gave up the ghost.

When we rent a car in America we assume the tank to be full. Not in Tanzania. They give you about enough to get you out of the lot, but I didn't know that and hadn't checked. The gas gauge registered full when I left, but it didn't work. When I checked it later at Olduvai Gorge the tank turned out to be empty.

So there I was, with my car totally stalled and unable to think about what to do next. The car was as hot as an oven, so I couldn't stay in—but it was dangerous to leave it.

Fortunately, there were no lions in sight, and I knew that big cats sleep during the midday sun and prowl in the cool of the evening. To make matters even more dramatic, I could see dry animal bones scattered around the car—ominous portents of the fate that awaited me when my turn came.

I ate my packed lunch, started rationing my last bottle of water, and tried to think of a plan of action. None suggested themselves.

Then two tall figures seemed to appear on the horizon. I say, "seemed to appear" because in the sunlight that was shimmering from the heat I thought they might be mirages. I looked again and they seemed to move, so I started toward them. But with every step I took they retreated. I quickened my pace, making frantic gestures of distress, and they gradually slowed their pace and allowed me to catch up with them.

They turned out to be two Masai warriors, disconcertingly tall, who wore nothing but spears taller than themselves and strips of flapping cloth that covered their shoulders and did their best to ward off the scorching sun.

What then could I do?

I was in human company but without words to communicate. *Something* had to be done! I seized one of them by the wrist and marched him back to my dysfunctional car with his companion in tow. This seemed to amuse them, and why not? What had my pile of junk have to do with *them*?

The two of them conversed, but then they started to leave, a prospect that terrified me. I seized one of my hostage's wrists to stall him.

He and his friend were my only lifeline, and I couldn't allow it to be severed. They laughed and talked, and then one of them turned away and began running off toward the distant horizon in that beautiful long noble stride of the Masai runners, leaving his hostage with me.

When the first runner returned a little later he had a small boy in tow, who knew a few words of English, though "Hello" and "Goodbye" was about the extent of it. Someone must have taught him those words. Hoping that he might understand me I pointed in several different directions, and asked, "School, school Where? Where?" I asked plaintively. The boy gave little sign of comprehension, and my hopes waned. But after conversing with his companions a little more, he and the man who had fetched him went off together, leaving me once again with my hostage.

About an hour later, they returned with ten adult cohorts. As the sun set that evening, one of the most bizarre scenes that had ever unfolded on the Serengeti Plains took place. A team of Masai warriors were pushing a dilapidated Renault across on the trackless Serengeti Plains with a lost American scholar sitting comfortably at the wheel. My human propellers were pushing me out of danger, turning the experience into a great lark, chattering and laughing at the same time and sounding like a flock of happy birds.

My first thought was, "*Who is listening?*" This was followed immediately by, "*Who cares?*" because my newfound friends were having such a good time helping me.

Six miles across the Plains they pushed me in the old Renault where they finally delivered me to the putative "school" that the boy had actually understood in his own way. It turned out to be a building at Olduvai Gorge, where a decade earlier Louis and Mary Leakey, along with their son Richard, had discovered the tooth, which the press heralded as the discovery that "set the human race back a million years."

In those days the Leakeys divided their year. For six months they excavated, and for the balance of the year they left the excavating to a crew of workmen headed by an overseer who could speak English, while they oversaw the Museum of Natural History in Nairobi.

When I arrived at the Gorge the first thing I told my host was that I wanted to pay the Masai handsomely for saving my life, but knew that of course my travelers checks would be useless to them.

"So, please, will you reward them?" I suggested. "I will repay you." I never saw what my host actually presented them with, but the warriors wandered off chirping like happy birds.

Then I told the overseer my story. When he asked me what I proposed to do, I asked him how far we were from the highway and when he said two miles I said I would walk there and hitch a ride to the city. The next day, I promised him, I would return with a tow truck that could transport the car back to the rental agency in Dar es Salaam. It was then that he spoke the words that form the heading for this section of this chapter: "If you walk, the highway at this time of day you *must* be eaten by lions."

It sounded more like a command than a warning.

I decided to wait until morning.

At supper I slaked my thirst but not on what I was fed. I was ushered to the simple bungalow that the Leakeys lived in while they worked on site. That incredible day ended with me sleeping in Louis Leakey's cot, drinking the whiskey on the floor beside it, and cursing the two of them for their inhospitality in not being present to welcome me in person.

Incidentally, the press credited Louis with discovering the infamous tooth, but actually it was Mary who discovered it. I sent that correction to *Ms* magazine, but they didn't print it.

That encounter on the Serengeti left me with a profound sense of human connectedness. There we were, as different in every way— ethnically, linguistically, and culturally—as any two groups on our planet. Yet without a single word in common, we had connected. They understood my predicament and responded with a will—and just as important—with style.

That adventure taught me to beware of the differences that blind us to the unity that binds us.

HUSTON SMITH, AMERICAN HISTORIAN OF RELIGION

COLTRANE BY TWILIGHT

Gray, green
twilight blues.

Hollow trumpet climbs,
snare caresses drums.
Fingers curl over creamy keys,
notes twirl.

A pause:
lifetimes culminate.
Love begins with a sultry swirl,
ends with a stab.

Each sound slowly
darkens the blues,
which touch
then meld into one.

Time stops
and softly smiles.

ERIN BYRNE, AMERICAN WRITER

Then, we were in Nice. The sun, a big copper gong, smoldered high overhead in a wrapper of haze. The sea was a vitreous blue. We sat on deck chairs, our backs to the city—behind us, the Promenade des Anglais. A river of old people with hair like batting, complexions like broken geraniums, drifted by. On the other side of the promenade, a seawall of multi-floored buildings rose, curved around the coast, chalky fronts peering out over the Mediterranean Sea. Further down the beach, the tangle of trashcans, brown bodies, paper sacks and food crowded in a ghetto of flesh and debris. Nice, like a thick grenadine, trickled over us.

We squandered an afternoon at the water's edge. Yellow buoys bobbed on the flickering surface. A young fisherman sat on the end of the pier, his pole dipping half-heartedly into the shallows. The sun fell behind the dome of the magnificent Hotel Negresco. A flag mounted upon the rotunda seemed to clutch at it as it went. It was muggy, still warm. Soon enough, we would be on another train, in another *couchette* lit, on our way to Geneva. The humidity sheathed us like a second skin. The night air brought with it a separate chill.

"Lawrence, are you cold?" I asked, noticing the goose flesh on my own bare arms.

He didn't respond. He was writing busily in his journal, no doubt stringing together metaphors, similes to describe the sun. He pointed to his subject of study, that red-shelled beetle creeping down from the sky. On the beach, sunbathers clumped together, trying to share one another's warmth. They refused to relinquish their hold on day even as it slipped out from under them. The first artificial lights twinkled on.

Umbrellas closed. The last sun worshippers wound themselves around and around in sweaters and towels. At our backs, the city awakened, gaily decked in tiaras of light. We walked along the darkening lip of sand. My hands fumbled under Lawrence's clothes, hunting for remnants of fever, the shreds of warmth hidden within him.

Lawrence slid his hands into my jeans.

"Ew," he said with a shudder. "Cold ass."

"Cold ass, hot snatch," I said smartly, moving his hands.

Point of ignition, I could feel the flame leap.

"C'mon, Lawrence," I dared, "Let's make a fire."

His mouth was already on mine. I squeezed my eyes shut and held on, clinging like a drowning woman, wanting to bring him down, too. I tried to push through the rack of his ribs, press toward his heart, toward the tented wings of his lungs. It was his breathing that filled the cavity of my chest. I felt soothed by his warmth, the rhythm of his hips. His life was a river that snaked into me, ran the length of my limbs, spilled heat.

Later, his arms still around me, we sat for a while, like nesting boxes, braced against nightfall, looking out toward the shadowed horizon. A few feet away, the cold sea sucked at the land. Music whined, petulant, from one of the clubs. It hung plaintively over us, for a moment, wafted

out over the black waves, dissolved.
  We fled inland, toward the trains.

LINDA WATANABE MCFERRIN, AMERICAN WRITER

YOU HAVE OPENED A SECRET TONIGHT

You have opened a secret tonight
That is the night itself, where black,
Dervish-outcast crows dissolve into
Joy, gone to fly with the white falcon.

MEVLANA RUMI,
PERSIAN POET AND MYSTIC, 1207–1273
TRANSLATED FROM THE PERSIAN BY COLEMAN BARKS

LOVE AT THE EDGE OF THE GRAND CANYON

I was seven when my great-grandmother reached ninety. She was a beautiful woman, with large violet eyes, exquisitely groomed white hair, and magnificent hands, veined and transparent, which she enhanced with antique rings. She gave me one, an oblong amethyst, set in heavy gold, which I love more and more as I get older. She wore brocade dresses with lace petticoats. The shoes on her little feet always matched her satin hair bands. She liked to talk to me. I liked to listen. She told me many things. She told me once about a love affair she had years earlier "on the edge of the Grand Canyon." She was much younger then, she explained, only seventy-four. "On the very edge," she repeated in her crystal clear, yet most soft voice. "It was very romantic. I looked straight down the canyon walls-a thousand miles below. We were passionate then and unafraid, being young."

At the time, I had no idea what she was talking about. By the time I understood, I imagined my exquisite and delicate great-grandmother in a passionate embrace with a mysterious stranger on the very rim of the Grand Canyon, while a sunset of glorious oranges and golds spread across a darkening vastness.

Birds would have called to each other as they settled in their nests, their soul-filled evening songs as tender as any my great-grandmother sang to me. In my mind, the sky changed to green, then red and purple, finally setting on the dark blue of unpolluted might.

Meanwhile, a moon rose and shadows got darker. Single mesas

were etched in silver, and the canyon rim itself was a rippling ribbon of black, silver, and sand, as far as the eye could reach. Mirror-smooth "a thousand miles below," a river reflected the moon and the stars, which came out, first one by one, then as if thrown by handfuls, until bucketsful were tumbled across the sky to laugh above the lovers. Holding hands, the lovers, I imagined, dangled their feet over the edge, rapt in the beauty. Then, when there was only black and silver and silence all around, they made love.

I believed the story, and so I always believed that life is extravagantly beautiful, slightly risky, and continuously love filled.

Also precarious.
And a bit sandy.
Not for the faint-hearted.
In a word, mythic.

Many years later, I was on my honeymoon with my new husband, Alexander Eliot, driving across the West. Not being familiar with the speeds at which one could travel in those days, we had not planned upon reaching the Grand Canyon until the middle of the next day, but, by late afternoon, we found ourselves at the entrance to Grand Canyon National Park and decided to stay the night.

We followed the signs to the central complex, where a new hotel blazed in the center of what seemed to be a parking lot. Tall street lamps glowed down the cars of many colors blocking off the late afternoon light. Coffee shops were already filled, the smell of fried food obliterating the fragrance of pines and cedars. People scurried with suitcases, calling sharply to children. No birds sang. Newly arriving travelers, all with reservations, crowded the lobby. The harried man at the desk was sorry, but there were no more rooms.

"I know that hotels always have an extra room for an emergency," Alex said. "Say a VIP arrives unexpectedly. Give us that room and we'll pay for it." Alex was in no mood to drive any further.

"Sir, that is not the case. We would give you a proper room if we had one. But we have only one room left, one we never rent anymore. It is in the Old Inn, and people didn't like it, so we don't bother to show it."

"Sounds perfect," Alex said.

A bellboy called ahead and then, gathering our bags, led us over to the Old Inn. We followed him through its lovely old lobby and then down the corridors to the back of the building. We were quite disoriented by the time we reached our room—apartment—I should say, with rooms worthy of the Grand Canyon. The bedroom was the size of an ordinary ballroom, and the bathroom your run-of-the-mill living room. The tub itself was about seven feet long and four feet deep—a fitting object of sculpture.

Everything was ready for us by the time we got there: large towels in the bathroom, bed turned down, curtains pulled. A fire had been lit and was burning cheerfully. The room was large but had a cozy feel to it: green and white chintz and natural wood and wicker furniture. An antique silver mirror glowed resplendent over the dressing table. The bed was big enough for five.

"Nothing wrong with this," I said.

The bellboy silently accepted the tip, put another log on the fire and left.

The first thing was a hot bath. It took some time to fill, but soon the heat was loosening the tensions of the day. After a while, I remembered the sunset. The window was right there bedside the tub. I hardly had to move to pull back the curtain and look out: sky, orange and gold, shot through with giant splashes of green and purple. A star. A half moon, green in the golden air. I looked over to the far side of the Grandest Canyon of them all. The edge was still visible. My eyes climbed slowly down to a silvery ribbon, running in the already black of the canyon bottom. I got up on my knees to see better and gasped.

Grabbing a thick towel, I tumbled out of the bath and ran into the bedroom. Our bed was set right against an enormous window. I jumped on it and threw open the curtains. Sure enough, the bed, too, was right over the canyon.

I knew immediately that this had been Great-Grandmother's room all those years ago.

Speechless, I beckoned Alex. The pull of the dreadful height got to us. We lay on our stomachs to look. There was no rim on this side—nothing between us and the bottom. Only an awesome down.

"Down a thousand miles," as Great-Grandmother had said.

Alex looked at me, and I looked at him.

If Great-Grandmother could, we can: our eyes agreed.

We left the curtain open that evening on the very edge of the Grand Canyon.

Jane Winslow Eliot,
Spanish-American writer, activist, 1928–2012

Steve and Martha were nearly 80 years old as they reached their 50th anniversary. Although they didn't look as sexy as they once did, the night time is kind in this regard and they determined to make love on the night of their Golden Anniversary. But Martha knew Steve would have trouble getting an erection so she sent him in advance to see a shaman who lived in the nearby woods and was reputed to have powerful medicine.

The old shaman gave Steve a potion and, putting a hand on Steve's shoulder warned "This is strong medicine. You take only a teaspoon full and then you say '1-2-3.' When you do that you will become as strongly erect as you have ever been and make love as long as you want." Steve was encouraged. As he walked away he turned and asked, "How do I stop the medicine from working?" The shaman responded "Your partner must say '1-2-3-4,' but when she does the medicine's effect will end at once and not work again until the next full moon."

On the evening of their anniversary, as the darkness settled in through the windows, Steve went into the bedroom, took a spoonful of the medicine and invited Martha to join him. When she came in he took off his clothes, said "1-2-3" and immediately got an erection. Martha was very pleased and excited, and as she quickly started taking her clothes off asked, "What was the '1-2-3' for?"

And that is the reason we should never end a sentence with a preposition. We could end up in the dark with a dangling participle.

JAMES BOTSFORD, AMERICAN LAWYER-POET

NIGHT FEED

When at midnight my wife turns the shield
of her back to me, feeds the baby, then whispers,
It's OK, shh, there's another one, it's OK,
as she lifts him on her shoulder a moment
before giving him to the other breast,
I can see his face up there dark from sleep.
The eyes glisten. More than that,
they shine with their own chemistry:
phosphorescence, the lambency at night
of certain polyps, an urgent bio-luminescence
with its own laws, its own necessities—
things more important than my own sleepy head
already in its prime, restless on the pillow.

HENRY SHUKMAN,
ENGLISH POET AND WRITER, FORMER TROMBONIST, ZEN TEACHER

PART II:

NIGHTHAWKS

*Unconsciously, probably, I was
painting the loneliness of a large city.*

— EDWARD HOPPER

D usk darkens. Night falls. Nighthawks take flight. While the opening section reveled in the sheer beauty of twilight, this second section revels in what it's possible *to do* in the middle of the night. Here we celebrate the poetry of work in the reflections of an insomniac, astronomer, poet, arctic explorer, photographer, doctor, naturalist, all-night disc jockey, musician, pilot, soldier, baseball historian, travel writer, and many other nighthawks. These are nightbound souls who refuse to go willingly into the arms of Morpheus. They would rather defy the urge to sleep and rest and instead burn the midnight oil and stay awake as long as possible to finish the unfinished business of the day—or get inspired to begin something bold and new.

For me, this caliber of observation of the night world is exemplified by a story I heard about Sir Arthur Conan Doyle when I was living in London in the mid-1970s. It seems that one evening in

New York City, in 1894, a crafty cabbie picked up Conan Doyle and spoke to him like a long lost friend all the way to the hall where the author, who had mythologized the powers of observation and the the supremacy of reason in his creation of Sherlock Holmes, was slated to give an evening lecture. Instead of a fare, the cabbie asked for a ticket to the lecture. Baffled, Conan Doyle asked, "How on earth did you recognize me?"

"If you will excuse me," the cabbie replied, "Your coat lapels are badly twisted downward, where they have been grasped by the pertinacious New York reporters. Your hair has the Quakerish cut of a Philadelphia barber, and your hat, battered at the brim in front, shows where you have tightly grasped it in the struggle to stand your ground at a Chicago literary function. Your right shoe has a large block of Buffalo mud just under the instep; the odor of a Utica cigar hangs about your clothing. And, of course, the labels on your case give a full account of your recent travels, the plaque reading: 'Conan Doyle.'"

"Excellent, excellent," Conan Doyle cried out, happy that someone had been reading him and his books so attentively. "And so elementary, my dear boy. I did not observe, and you did."

The contributors reveal a kind of melancholic exultation in the knowledge that while the rest of the world is sleeping they are observing and making deductions about the night world in a way that would make Doyle's Sherlock Holmes proud. This ambiguous relationship to the night is explored in art critic Alexander Eliot's interview with Edward Hopper and discussion of his iconic *Nighthawks*. The painting shows four quiet people lingering in an all-night diner that hauntingly portrays the ambiguity of modern life, in all its neon-amplified beauty and loneliness.

Twenty five hundred years ago, Sappho, the tenth muse, wrote of young women singing at night about their lovers, which may be the acme of the celebration of the night. In the fifteenth century, Galileo turned his telescope and the world's attention to what is "splendid" about the night sky, an observation echoed centuries later by Rachel Carson and the Milwaukee poet laureate, Antler, who describes the influence of the campfire to spark in us the urge to "stay up all night" with our friends and lovers and "renew the pledges." Similarly, in John Muir's journals we find in the stunning beauty of a glacier the inspiration to write the night through. In *Alone*, one of the great adventure stories of the twentieth century, Richard E. Byrd describes how he kept his sanity during six months of isolation at the South Pole—steadfastly making scientific observations, or what he charmingly called his "obs" in his Scottish shorthand. And the nineteenth-century English poet Matthew Tate provides us with a rare glimpse into the subterranean world of coal miners, one of the most classic commentaries ever written about work. Mahatma Gandhi distils centuries of night wisdom when he writes in an essay how he "can see in the midst of darkness." In his seminal travel book, *The Songlines*, Bruce Chatwin speculates on the universal fear of darkness that has plagued human beings since the days on the savanna. War historian Stanley Weintraub paints a haunting picture of the sacred dimension of the night in his story about English,

French, and German soldiers who suspended hostilities in No Man's Land, in 1914, and sang Christmas carols. The artist and composer Stuart Balcomb evokes the silken darkness of his college darkroom and its lifelong effects on his creative efforts. The Paris-based photographer Richard Beban calls up a Wolfman Jack-like evocation of working as an all-night disc jockey at KSAN, in San Francisco, in the 1970s, a piece he describes as "an attempt at songwriting, meant to be set to music." After we flip over his record, we hear from Miles Davis who once admitted that he was trying to get the sound of the dark country roads of Arkansas into his trumpet. The American-Norwegian photographer Mikkel Aaland recounts a strange dream that allows us to appreciate the moiré of night and never be certain of what we see; other than that, as he says, it reflects our "obsession with time"—a good night's work. Nikos Kazantzakis's rendering of his iconic hero, Zorba, brings the man of fire to life one night, never a man so fiery; the moonlight helped the teacher see him better, as one in accord with the universe. Bill Haney throws a curving metaphor in "Night Game," an account of one of the first games ever played at Briggs Stadium, in Detroit, under the flood lights. Despite being wary of playing ball at night, the Tigers and Yankees swatted 11 home runs, and the hometeam prevailed, 10-9. So much for not being able to see the ball at night.

All the shadow-fretted themes of this part of the book come together in Pico Iyer's essay on nightwalking in Manila, which he describes with an unmistakable sense of awe and wonder at the sights and sounds of the teeming capital city. His observations are rooted in what he calls *monogashi*, which he describes in *The Painted Word* as referring "to the beauty of things that are dying, the sweetness of sadness, the mingled quality of life, and the way that dusk can be evocative and haunting precisely because it speaks for the end of things, the coming of the dark."

In his magisterial *The Library at Night*, Alberto Manguel describes the room of books in his fifteenth-century French home, Le Presbytère: "In the dark, with the windows lit and the rows of books glittering, the library is a closed space, a universe of self-serving rules that pretend to replace or translate those of the shapeless universe beyond." The extract I have chosen here reveals Manguel's admiration for two great readers, Machiavelli and Montaigne, and his own predilection for writing by day and reading by night. "Reading is, in this sense, a ritual of rebirth.... But at night, when the library lamps are lit, the outside world disappears and nothing but the space of books remains in existence."

This squinting in the soul is for true vision, learning to see the invisible. For we strive always to see in the dark; we hope for light through poems and prayers; and we pay any cost to wedge open a crack between the worlds if it means learning one new thing about ourselves. These night writers provide an antidote to the search for enlightenment, which is the daily discovery of endarkenment, an acknowledgement of our need for both light and darkness. Rather than grinching to us about what is missing in the day world, they are beguiling us about what can be found in the shadow-fretted night.

Night
Virgins
will all night long sing
of the love between you and your bride
in her violet robe.

Wake and call out young men
Of your age,
And tonight we shall sleep less than
The bright-voiced nightingale

Sappho, Greek poet, 625-570 B.C.E.
Translated from the ancient Greek
by Willis Barnstone

"If you could see the earth illuminated when you were in a place as dark as night, it would look to you more splendid than the moon."

— GALILEO GALILEI

Galileo Galilei, a most humble servant of Your Serene Highness.... Now appear before You with a new contrivance of glasses [*occhiale*], drawn from the most recondite speculations of perspective, which render visible objects so close to the eye and represent them so distinctly that those that are distant, for example, nine miles appear as though they were only one mile distant. This is a thing of inestimable benefit for all transactions and undertakings, maritime or terrestrial, allowing us at sea to discover at a much greater distance than usual the hulls and sails of the enemy, so that for two hours or more we can detect him before he detects us.

*Galileo Galilei, letter to the Doge (chief magistrate of Venice) explaining the practical uses of the telescope, giving the Senate sole rights to the new device, and asking for tenure at the university. He received tenure, although the accompanying doubling of his salary to 1,000 florins per year did not start until his current contract ended and excluded further pay increases, 31 August 1609.

THE NIGHT IS MUCH MORE ALIVE

8 September 1888

My dear Theo,

Thank you a thousand times for your kind letter and the 300 francs it contained—after some weeks of worries I've just had a much better one. And just as worries don't come singly, nor do joys, either... I'd paint the [the lodging-house keeper's] whole filthy old place as a way of getting my money back. Well, to the great delight of the lodging-house keeper, the postman whom I've already painted, the prowling night-visitors and myself, for 3 nights I stayed up to paint, going to bed during the day. It often seems to me that the night is much more alive and richly colored than the day. Now as for recovering the money paid to the landlord through my painting, I'm not making a point of it, because the painting is one of the ugliest I've done. It's the equivalent, though different, of the potato eaters.

Later on, when I've taken those experiments further, the sower will still be the first attempt in that genre. The night café is a continuation of the sower, as is the head of the old peasant and of the poet, if I manage to do the latter painting. It's a color, then, that isn't locally true from the realist point of view of trompe l'oeil, but a color suggesting some emotion, an ardent temperament...

Anyway, soon—tomorrow or the day after—I'll write to you

again on this subject and will reply to your letter, sending you *croquis* [sketches] of the night café... Thank you once again for the money sent. If I was first going to look for another place, isn't it likely that then there would be new expenses in that, at least equivalent to the costs of moving? And moreover, would I find better right away? I'm very glad indeed to be able to furnish my house, and that can only help me get on. So many thanks and good handshake; till tomorrow.

Ever yours,
Vincent

VINCENT VAN GOGH, DUTCH PAINTER, 1853-1890
LETTER SENT TO HIS BROTHER, THEO

CAMPFIRE TALK

Lonely, contemplating suicide?
Go alone into the forest, find a clearing,
Gather wood, build a fire, stay up all night
    with the fire and the stars.
Have a little blackberry brandy as your telescope
    to bring the stars closer in.
The sound of the fire, the smell of the fire,
The light and heat of the fire
    will help you, heal you.
A campfire's a Paleolithic experience
    we can all still have.

Renew the pledge of brotherhood round the fire.
Renew the pledge of sisterhood round the fire.
Hold hands in a circle and each make
    the sacred vow and pledge
And then silence, silence
    and the fire,
But really you're alone,
You only imagined your friends
    and lovers near,
Only imagined all the poets you love
    holding hands round the fire as one.

The flames recede,
The logs fall in among themselves,
Sparks fly up, a puff of smoke, a sigh,
    the fire dies down.
The cold creeps in and you draw nearer
    the ebbing flame,
And then the embers, the embers glowing
    softly red
While above the startling stars
    and forest smell rush in
    as eyes adjust to the dark.

The towering ancient trees nearby
Cease being lit
    by flickering light.
Warm your hands one last time
    over the dying fire.
Remain. Remain long
    after the fire is out,
Long after the cold creeps in.
Look up at the stars
    longer than you ever have
    and maybe ever will.

Renew the pledge of friendship round the fire.
Renew the pledge of love around the fire.
Make the vow of vows under the stars.
Renew, renew around the campfire
  in the wilderness under a wilderness of stars.
And then silence, silence and the expiring fire
  and the silent continuous movement
  of Stars and Earth in Space
Till the embers fade away—
  and with the first light of day
  shoulder your pack and head forth.

ALONE WITH THE STARS

One summer night, out on a flat headland, all but surrounded by the waters of the bay, the horizons were remote and distant rims on the edge of space. Millions of stars blazed in darkness, and on the far shore a few lights burned in cottages. Otherwise there was no reminder of human life. My companion and I were alone with the stars: the misty river of the Milky Way flowing across the sky, the patterns of the constellations standing out bright and clear, a blazing planet low on the horizon. It occurred to me that if this were a sight that could be seen only once in a century, this little headland would be thronged with spectators. But it can be seen many scores of nights in any year, and so the lights burned in the cottages and the inhabitants probably gave not a thought to the beauty overhead. And because they could see it almost any night, perhaps they never will.

RACHEL CARSON,
AMERICAN WRITER, MARINE BIOLOGIST,
CONSERVATIONIST, 1904–1964

The Ohen:ton Karihwatehkwen is the Mohawk "Thanksgiving Address" said before any social, ceremonial, or political gathering. It consists of eighteen parts in which different elements of the universe are formally acknowledged and given gratitude. Among those elements are earth, plants, animals, winds, sun, moon and stars. For the stars the speaker will say the following:

> *We give thanks to the Stars who are spread across the sky*
> *like jewelry. We see them in the night helping the Moon*
> *to light the darkness and bringing dew to the gardens and*
> *growing things. When we travel at night they guide us*
> *home. With our minds gathered as one we send greetings*
> *and thanks to all the Stars.*

The word for *stars* in Mohawk is *o:tsis:tah* (pronounced oh:jees:dah), which has the same root as "fire" *o:tsi:se:re* (pronounced Oh:jee:se:leh). Stars are the ultimate hearth fires of the Iroquois, whose point of origin for the human species is traced to a specific cluster called the "Seven Dancers," or the Pleiades.

The first being is called *Iotsitsisen* (pronounced yo:ji:ji:sen), the Skywoman, who came from a place in the Pleiades region on a beam of light. Her name means "Mature Flower," and she was one of other beings of light, the Skypeople. From her world she descended to earth, piercing a cloud-draped world which had become inundated by a great flood. She brought with her the seeds of plants considered sacred by the Iroquois. These were strawberries *(fragaria vesca)*, *Kohnniiohet-sera* (guh:ni:yoh:het:se:lah), a plant with curative powers for the heart and the berry consumed by the Iroquois upon death and along the celestial pathway back to the Seven Dancers. The others were tobacco *(nicotiana rustica)*, called *ohiokwehonwhe* (oh:yo:gwe:hohn:weh) and corn (zia mays): *ohneste* (oh:nes:teh). Together the three form critical components of Iroquois social, spiritual, and ceremonial life.

Tobacco is of unique importance. It is generally grown by men and is not for casual use. The most potent, aromatic, and sacred species is a broad-leafed, dark green plant, which grew from the head of the Skywoman. Because of this the Iroquois are able to use tobacco to communicate directly with the spirits once the dried leaves are put into a fire and with the appropriate words. Rarely is this form of tobacco smoked directly, as it is very pungent and has a harsh, raw taste. It may be tempered by mixing it with other plants. Strawberries came from the heart of the Skywoman, while corn is said to have grown from her breasts, hence the Iroquois custom of planting in mounds.

The origin of all three plants can be traced to Central and South America. The Iroquois stories as to our origins follow a similar path, migrating like the plants from the southwest to the northeast. The common beginning place is that region which is believed to be the point of entry by human beings into the western hemisphere, specifically the highlands of Central America.

The alignment of stars determines when the Iroquois plant and hold the most important of ceremonies, called *Shatekohsehrhen* (sha:de:goh:seh:lehn) or Midwinter. This seven-day communal ritual of thanksgiving marks the lengthening of days. It takes place in the longhouse, the Iroquois ceremonial building, five days after the first new moon following the winter solstice and when the Pleiades are at a certain number of degrees above the eastern horizon.

Stars were also used in planting, with their alignment determining when some seeds were placed into the soil. Stars also marked distance and time while serving as guides for travelers and hunters. Stars are also said to bring about the dew which moistens plants throughout the night and may determine the fate of human beings. Upon physical death the spirit-*ahtunhets* (ah:duhn:hets) leaves the body and hovers nearby. A series of rituals are held to persuade the spirit to leave this earth and begin its journey back to the Skyworld. Through a series of detachments the soul follows the star path (Milky Way) on a year-long venture during which it is escorted by spiritual guides. Once there, the soul contributes its life experiences to the divine light and may opt to return to the earth to serve as a guardian to the living. There are many star stories in the rich oral traditions of the Iroquois. There are tales of celestial bears, of young people ascending to the stars, of spirits who come from the heavens to give direction to the people. These night-time fires continue as vital elements in contemporary Iroquois life.

DOUGLAS GEORGE-KANENTIINO, IROQUOIS JOURNALIST

GLACIERS BY STARLIGHT

We gathered a lot of fossil wood and after supper made a big fire, and as we sat around it the brightness of the sky brought on a long talk with the Indians about the stars; and their eager, child-like attention was refreshing to see as compared with the deathlike apathy of weary town-dwellers, in whom natural curiosity has been quenched in toil and care and poor shallow comfort.

After sleeping a few hours, I stole quietly out of the camp, and climbed the mountain that stands between the two glaciers. The ground was frozen, making the climbing difficult in the steepest places; but the views over the icy bay, sparkling beneath the stars, were enchanting. It seemed then a sad thing that any part of so precious a night had been lost in sleep. The starlight was so full that I distinctly saw not only the berg-filled bay, but most of the lower portions of the glaciers, lying pale and spirit-like amid the mountains. The nearest glacier in partic-ular was so distinct that it seemed to be glowing with light that came from within itself. Not even in dark nights have I ever found any diffi-culty in seeing large glaciers; but on this mountain-top, amid so much ice, in the heart of so clear and frosty a night, everything was more or less luminous, and I seemed to be poised in a vast hollow between two skies of almost equal brightness.

This exhilarating scramble made me glad and strong and I rejoiced that my studies called me before the glorious night succeeding so glorious a morning had been spent!

JOHN MUIR,
SCOTTISH-AMERICAN NATURALIST AND MEMOIRIST, 1838–1914

ALONE IN THE ARCTIC NIGHT

April 22, 1914

...It is now close to midnight. In a moment I shall go to bed. I know exactly what I shall do. With a pencil stroke, I shall cross this day off the calendar; then fetch snow and alcohol tablets for the morning tea, and, finally, make sure that the instruments are functioning properly. This inspection over, I shall take a quick glance from the hatch to see whether anything unusual is happening in the auroral department. After battening down the trapdoor, I shall undress, turn down the pressure lantern, put out the fire, open the door, and jump for the sleeping bag, leaving the storm lantern burning over my head. That part of the routine is automatic. As long as heat remains in the shack, I shall read; tonight it will be the second volume of the *Life of Alexander*, which I've nearly finished. That part is by choice. When my hands turn numb, I'll reach up and blow out the lantern, but not until I have first made sure that the flashlight is somewhere in the sleeping bag, where my body will keep the battery warm.

I don't try to force myself to sleep, as I sometimes do at home. My whole life here in a sense is an experiment in harmony, and I let the bodily processes achieve a natural equilibrium. As a rule, it doesn't take me long to go to sleep. But a man can live a lifetime in a few half-dreaming moments of introspection between going to bed and falling asleep: a lifetime reordered and edited to satisfy the ever-changing demands of the mind.

RICHARD E. BYRD,
ARCTIC EXPLORER, AVIATOR, 1888–1957

A NIGHT IN AN IGLOO

The call of the wild has a peculiar power over some psyches, I pondered, snow-stuck halfway through the low tunnel into an Arctic igloo. *What, O Great Sky Father, am I doing here?*

Here was a straggle of houses along ice-bound Grise Fjord, northernmost nonmilitary settlement on the globe, south tip of Ellesmere Island, 721 miles north of the Arctic Circle and 959 from the North Pole. At 11 p.m., in the limp light that serves as May's excuse for darkness at this latitude, I had waddled over the sea-ice from the perfectly adequate prefab Grise Fjord Lodge just to play Eskimo. I was as bulbous as Bibendum, the Michelin man.

Squeezed into ski gear, we eight "explorers" had hesitated in Resolute Bay, Northern Territories, at the outfitters of High Arctic International Services to be stuffed like sausages into U.S.-inspired military "outer" gear: powder-pants, parkas with fur-rimmed hoods, all-obscuring down masks, mittens larger than Yogi Berra's catcher's mitt, Canadian

Caribou boots.

Prone on my paunch halfway into the igloo, I recalled a conversation with my ophthalmologist: "Will my contact lenses freeze at the Pole?" I had asked. "Not," he had answered gleefully, "until your eyes do!"

Mushing into the igloo, I stripped down to layers of long underwear and socks and bundled into my well-chilled bag. Hist! Through the tunnel entered expedition leader Mike Dunn, photographer Wolfgang Kaehler, and a pretty young teacher with a frigid smile. "We didn't want you to have *all* the fun," she groaned.

Dunn carved ice cubes out of the wall, popped them into paper cups, then splashed in Johnny Walker Red. "Scotch and *snowda!*" he pronounced.

Sleeping was O.K.; waking at six a.m. and clumping out of my cocoon into the snow-shell at eleven degrees below zero was not. My fingers tried with only partial success to dress me; they refused entirely to touch the heavy zippers of the Arctic pants or to tighten the laces on my boots. As properly clothed as they would permit, I stumbled across the ice toward the lodge that looked, through glazed eyes, like Lake Como's Villa d'Este.

No hot water. The pipes had frozen overnight. I washed my face and contact lenses in melted snow.

"How do you feel?" Dunn grinned.

"A little like Nanookie of the North," I sighed.

GEORGIA HESSE, AMERICAN SCRIBE

"Jackson Pollack and Willem de Kooning have nothing to say." After delivering that totally unjust judgment, Edward Hopper paused for a full moment or more, staring down at the floor between his shoes. "If they did," he concluded at last, "they wouldn't know how to say it."

"Both men paint images of flux," I suggested. "You can read whatever you like into those seismic openings of theirs. Exciting stuff."

"Humph!" Hopper said. That was his usual style of conversation. Never had I known so laconic a man.

We were in his Manhattan home: a fourth-floor walk-up at Number Three Washington Square North. The artist occupied the straight chair beside the old etching press he employed as a hat-rack. The tall windows at his back were violet with winter evening light, crossed by yellow lamplight reflections from within and flying snow outside.

"It's not hard to paint a design," Hopper told me dolefully. "Nor to paint a representation of something you can see. But to express a thought in painting—that is hard. Why? Because thought is fluid. What you put on canvas is concrete, and this tends to direct the thought. The more you put on canvas, the less of your original thought remains."

That was by far the longest and most complex statement I had ever heard from Hopper's lips. Hunching forward in his chair he raised his right hand to eye-level. His eyes were nearly crossed with concentration upon an invisible something beyond his fingertips. He made me see it also: an imaginary paintbrush. Very carefully, now, the artist moved as if to touch the brush-tip to an imaginary canvas. He was doing fine until, at the moment of seeming contact, an invisible outside force joggled his elbow.

Getting into the spirit of things, I gasped with concern. Hopper sat back again, deadpan.

Born to a storekeeping family in Nyack, New York, Hopper doggedly pursued his art career with almost no encouragement from any quarter. Like diamonds, this man's high art was produced under blind, stony pressure. Until the age of forty, he made a meager living as a commercial illustrator. "I'd walk around the block a couple of times before going in," he once confessed, "wanting the job for money and at the same time hoping to hell I wouldn't get the lousy thing."

Gravity and sparingness are qualities deep in the Puritan grain. Emily Dickinson possessed them; so did Charles Sheeler, Robert Frost, and Georgia O'Keeffe. But Edward Hopper was perhaps the gravest and sparest of the lot. His chirpy wife, Jo, did the smiling and chatting for them both.

Not until 1955, when he was in his seventies, did Hopper begin to receive the attention his non-commercial art had always merited. In that year he was awarded a Gold Medal for Painting by the American Academy of Arts and Letters. There was unconcealed bitterness in Hopper's one-word acceptance speech:

"*Thankyou.*"

"Recognition doesn't mean so much," the old gentleman confided to me the next day. "You never get it when you need it."

Paintings are supposed to be silent, of course. Some are more so than others. Hopper's have a bell-jar sort of silence about them. Not a sound, and yet you feel that if you were to touch a Hopper canvas with a tuning-fork it might well produce a barely audible vibration. His whole oeuvre seethes with low-voltage electric charges. It coruscates with a paradoxically dark brilliance.

"In every work of genius we recognize our own rejected thoughts. They come back to us with a certain alienated majesty." So Ralph Waldo Emerson observed, and Hopper's paintings bear that out. He deflects our own rejected thoughts back upon ourselves, with interest. Something which one had glimpsed a hundred times in passing from the corner of one's eye, or thought about a thousand times without ever pausing to reconsider, proves arresting after all.

Tearless nostalgia, the ache of loneliness, and finally the sense of romance just beyond reach inform Hopper's creative work. Each of his great canvases is narrowly but brilliantly staged, emptied of trivial details, and subtly distorted for dramatic impact. Each one tells a wordless story, but they're not illustrations of anything. Rather, they project strangely splendid insights into secret America.

Consider his *Nighthawks*, for example. This canvas, at the Chicago Art Institute, dates from 1942. We're out near a city corner, at the midnight hour, looking across the street and in through the plate glass window of a bright-lit fast-food joint. Hopper may well have passed a place like this on his frequent prowls around Greenwich Village, but he had his own means of transposing the scene to a legendary realm.

Thus he enlarged the empty pavement and the dark building, so that they seem broadly sweeping gestures of the night itself.

Contrastingly, the four figures at the counter inside appear small, crisp, courageous, and half-conscious of their isolation—marooned in light. The customer with his back to the street sits gazing across at the tensely close couple opposite and the priestly counterman in his starched white vestments. These four figures all display the same angular, dimly repressed body language.

This awkward stiffness is theirs, not Hopper's, yet the artist himself abjured gesture as a general rule. The flamboyance of the surrealists and the abstract expressionists alike repelled him. His own art has the stillness of a dreamer in bed. It doesn't express emotion; rather, it projects a mood peculiar to this artist alone. The mood is bleak and yet tender at the same time. It conveys a quality of casting about for one knows not what, like an inchworm at the end of a twig. "Self-seeking" was a synonym for selfishness in Hopper's time, and generally frowned upon. Yet Hopper insisted that he was in fact a "self-seeker."

Like every other midcentury artist of note, Hopper was naturally aware of psychoanalytic theory. It probably occurred to him that the four silently poised "Nighthawks" could symbolize distinct aspects of his own psyche. It's possible to read the painted scene as a mandala, a light-filled "center" in the dark of the painter's "unconscious" or dream-life. Thus the four figures could be interpreted as Jungian "archetypes": Shadow, Anima, Wise Old Man, and Ego, respectively. One might also see them as psychic functions: Feeling, Sensing,

Thinking, and Intuiting. Finally, they bring to mind the four "humors" of ancient lore: Sanguine, Phlegmatic, Melancholic, and Choleric.

But archetypes, functions, and humors are not self.

Looking at *Nighthawks*, I sense an invisible fifth participant who hovers on our side of the street. A passerby like us, he observes the action from the dark, and in through the plate glass, with appreciative and yet rather terrible detachment. Darkly shimmering, mercurial, and soon gone again is the artist's self, the actual nighthawk.

ALEXANDER ELIOT,
AMERICAN ART CRITIC AND MYTHOLOGIST

We had our annual Bonfire Night last night, June twenty-third, St John's Eve. It was a perfect evening. The wind, that had been blowing a gale earlier in the day, had died down and the rain had disappeared.

Our tradition on Inis Mór is to light the fire as the sun sets (around ten p.m.) and then to keep it lit until the sun rises again. Each village lights its own fire and we all gather around. It is the one time in the year when we come together as a village community. We bring food and drink, some of the children burn their end-of-year schoolbooks (!) and there is music and singing. There are fourteen villages on Inis Mór so that means fourteen bonfires. Our village is Mainistir. It is really just a townland with about twenty scattered houses. When we come together, we are celebrating both midsummer and our identity as the residents of Mainistir.

Our teenage girls had been baking all day, preparing treats of home-made biscuits and buns, to share at the bonfire. Tempting as they were, we were banned from touching them in advance of the evening's celebrations.

The Bonfire Night fire is lit at dusk on the longest day of the year. It is a tradition that goes back to pre-Christian times, celebrating midsummer, and has been kept alive by the local people without the input of priest or church, despite its Christian title. Nowadays, this practice occurs only along the western seaboard of Ireland in Connemara and the Aran Islands.

It is the job of the teenage boys to gather the waste timber in advance and to prepare the fire. These timber piles form into small mountains at the bonfire sites all across the island. While preparations begin days in advance, the fire must not be lit until the setting sun touches the horizon. It then must stay alight until the sun rises again very early the next morning.

The bonfire sites in each of the fourteen villages of Inis Mór have been used for these bonfires since time began. They are regarded as sacred sites, to be used for nothing else throughout the year. They are all on publicly accessible land, either on the roadside or on the shore next to the sea.

Dusk is an exciting time on Bonfire Night. As the day darkens, pillars of smoke begin to appear on the coastline of Connemara to the east and, to the south, above the silhouette of the two other Aran Islands, Inis Meáin and Inis Oirr. We then start looking for the signs of fires being lit on Inis Mór. Some, no doubt, will be bigger than others, but we want ours to be the biggest!

As we gather for the evening's celebrations, the fire is lit. It takes slowly at first, producing more smoke than flame. We sit around on the rocks. An old sofa is available for the older ones and there are also a few old mattresses. Later the sofa and mattresses will be burnt on the fire. As the fire gathers momentum, we have to move back or be scorched!

The music begins. Mary, with her pure clear voice, sings an Irish love song *as Gaeilge* (in the Irish language). Later her teenage daughter sings, and we see for the first time that her daughter has inherited the same beautiful singing voice. What a gift! The food is shared and everyone is in a very relaxed and friendly mood. Áine spontaneously takes on the role of M.C. for the night. Everybody joins in the singing.

Towards one a.m., it is time to bring the younger children home. The light is still in the sky towards the north. On this shortest night, it will never fully leave. It moves slowly from west to east behind the Twelve Bens and the Maamturks, silhouetting these mountains with a most amazing back light.

The younger people stay on. They are joined about an hour later by a whole new crowd of celebrants who have come up the hill from Joe Watty's pub in Kilronan, the next village. Part Two of the celebration begins. This time it goes on until six-thirty a.m., at which time, the new day sun has well risen and all that remains of the fire is a large pile of smouldering ashes and cinders. Even the sofa and mattresses are gone.

Bonfire night, the twenty-third of June, St John's Eve, is a celebration of midsummer and is therefore much older than Christianity or St John. The Christian connection, nonetheless, is interesting. The birthday of John the Baptist is the following day, June twenty-fourth. This is why Bonfire Night is also known as St John's Eve. Notice that this puts John's birthday on the summer solstice, while the birthday of Jesus is on the winter solstice.

The Christian calendar was not compiled until hundreds of years after the time of Jesus. Nobody knew the actual birthdays of either

Jesus or John the Baptist. However, if you look at the beginning of Luke's gospel, you will see that it states that these two "cousins" were born six months apart. So this six-month gap in the Christian calendar makes sense.

But why the two solstices? As the actual birthdays were unknown, there must have been a reason for choosing the dates we now have. The clue to this riddle is found in another part of Luke's gospel. In this passage, John as an adult is asked what he thinks of Jesus. His response includes the phrases: "He must increase, I must decrease."

Now if you apply those thoughts to the sun at the two solstices, this is exactly what happens. After John's birthday the sun decreases. After the birthday of Jesus, the sun increases.

This part of the Christian calendar may well have been a contribution by the Celtic monks. The Celtic monks were astronomers, very aware of the sun, moon and the cosmic cycles. Their version of Christianity was an inculturated variety, with the Christian story woven into their indigenous culture. In all indigenous cultures, it was the practice to project spiritual or mythological beliefs onto the environment and into the annual calendar of festivities. In this case, the reminders of these two significant birthdays were stitched into the solstices.

However, projecting spiritual and mythological narratives onto the natural environment only works when you operate within a local environment. It does not work on the global stage. The Roman church was intent on being a global corporation. Celebrating the birthday of Jesus on December twenty-fifth makes no sense in the southern hemisphere, where the date falls in midsummer. It turns the phrase "he must increase, I must decrease" on its head.

Bonfire Night on Inis Mór is a living, tangible manifestation of an ancient Celtic spiritual tradition that teaches us how to allow our spirituality to become rooted in a particular place. To celebrate Bonfire Night properly, you must come to Inis Mór!

DARA MOLLOY, IRISH WRITER AND CELTIC PRIEST

INIS MÓR NIGHT

There is a light out to sea.
Night is falling.
It is easy and slow—
a dimming
more than a darkness.
The rich yellow petals
of the gorse
have drunk deeply
of the sun all day long
and are now still glowing
in the twilight.
The waves curl endlessly,
Crashing against the cliffs
of Inis Meáin.

I feel the spirits of the dead around me
and I am unsettled.
The night welcomes something
that the sunlight dissipates.
Is it because
I am near the graveyard?
Or is it that the spirits
congregate

at the water's edge,
Wanting to be part of the curling waves
and the gently fading light?

I resist the urge to leave.
I know these spirits.
I have seen them live and die.
Éabha, at two,
curly-haired and smiling.
"Ná gort í," your mother cried
as they began to shovel the clay
onto your tiny white coffin.
Tom,
who sat for hours on the cliff top,
a string tied to your foot,
catching rock fish.
Seán Rose,
Captain.
Your home full of books,
Your head full of stories.
And Shauna,
Sixteen,
So ready to begin the life that ended.

These and many more.

I feel them around me.
Part of this place.
Part of this night.

I leave.
It seems indecent to linger.
My physical presence
pulsing as strongly
as the lighthouse beacon out to sea.
The night is theirs,
the night and the gathering darkness of Inis Mór.

TESS HARPER, IRISH POET AND WRITER

Who locked me
into this crazed man-made
stone brain
where the weathered
totempole jabs a blunt
finger at the Byzantine
mosaic dome

Under that ornate
golden cranium I wander
among fragments of gods, tarnished
coins, embalmed gestures
chronologically arranged,
looking for the EXIT sign

but in spite of the diagrams
at every corner, labeled
in red: YOU ARE HERE
the labyrinth holds me,

turning me around
the cafeteria, the washrooms,
a spiral through marble

Greece and Rome, the bronze
horses of China

then past the carved masks, wood and fur
to where 5 plaster Indians
in a glass case
squat near a dusty fire

and further, confronting me
with a skeleton child, preserved
in the desert air, curled
beside a clay pot and a few beads.

I say I am far
enough, stop here please
no more

but the perverse museum, corridor
by corridor, an idiot
voice jogged by a pushed
button, repeats its memories

and I am dragged to the mind's
dead end, the roar of the bone-
yard, I am lost

among the mastodons
and beyond: a fossil
shell, then

samples of rocks
and minerals, even the thundering
tusks dwindling to pin-
points in the stellar
fluorescent-lighted
wastes of geology.

Margaret Atwood, Canadian writer

CAFÉ DE NUIT

I'll wait for you in the Night Café,
in September, 1888,
on the first night of the three
Vincent painted from dusk until dawn
inside this *café de nuit* all night.

We'll sit close in the corner,
under the lemon lamp,
pure pool of yellow light,
in our own warm glow
amidst blood-red and green
terrible passions of humanity.

ERIN BYRNE, AMERICAN WRITER

THE DOMAIN OF THE NIGHT: THE DARKROOM

I spent a lot of my formative years in a very dark room. It measured 5 x 8 feet, when it wasn't totally dark, sometimes there was a dim red light. Yup, my dad was a photographer, and that "dark room" was a haven for me. One of my earliest memories (in the mid 1950s) is of standing on a little step stool, my nose just over the lip of the sink, seeing an image slowly emerge on the blank sheet of paper in the developer in the red light.

For a four-year-old it was pure magic—alchemy before my very eyes. Marilyn Monroe watched us coyly from her calendar on the wall. Then, through my boyhood and adulthood I spent many hours learning, developing, experimenting, and listening to music while printing hundreds of images. My busiest time in the darkroom was when I was in college, as I was a member of the yearbook staff. I used my dad's Rolleicord to shoot anything and everything, and then retreat to the darkroom to develop film and prints.

Just thinking back to those times I still sense the cozy, womb-like sanctuary feel of the room, and the almost holy sense of time/space/purpose; I still hear the sound of running water in the print washer, the enlarger ticking off its seconds of exposure, and the ever-present music softly providing a nocturnal soundtrack. I'd print for hours, day or night, but it didn't matter what time it was, because in the darkroom, time stopped and the world was asleep.

For me it was neither day nor night, for I was somewhere in the womb of the universe, where all was safe and everything was possible. And I was always surprised if it happened to still be daylight upon my emergence because for me the darkroom was and always will be the domain of the night.

STUART BALCOMB,
AMERICAN PUBLISHER, WRITER AND MUSICIAN

DEAD AIR / NIGHT RADIO

At three in the morning
the dreams are of falling
of being alone in the booth.

The microphone's missing
the record is ending
run out like the sap of his youth.

The deejay tastes panic
his movements are frantic
the records are in disarray.

The last note is ending
there's no use pretending
he'll have any smart words to say.

Chorus:

Some dream that they're naked
or they're giving a speech
grotesque humiliation
that salvation can't reach.

What is this mad precinct
to which we are summoned
in the darkness and terror of night?

As if pulled by instinct
we're all forced to come and
face the Stygian depths of our fright.

Our weak voices tremble
our thoughts all dissemble
we've fallen so far from the light.

The record is ending
he hunts for a new one
the alphabet's now disappeared.

There's no chance of finding
the cut that he's after—
dead air, just as he feared.

RICHARD BEBAN,
AMERICAN PHOTOJOURNALIST AND POET.

My life as a night owl began at an early age, in our big old, ten-bedroom, L-shaped farmhouse in Portland. I was put to bed at 9:00 and dozed off to the sounds of Rachmaninoff or Schubert or Debussy coming from my father's artist studio in the far corner of the second story of the house. Around midnight I would awaken when the music stopped, and listen for the door to open, smell the whiff of oil paint, and hear my dad shuffle quietly down the hall and down the stairs in his bedroom slippers, go into the kitchen, open the fridge, dish himself a big bowl of ice cream, pull up a chair at the kitchen table, and settle down to his book.

At this point I would put on my slippers, go down the hall to the kitchen, quietly close the door behind me so my mother wouldn't hear, get myself a spoon, and without a word, sit down beside him to share his ice cream and whatever he was reading that night. He would read aloud to me assuming characters and emotions and even sound effects with great hushed enthusiasm. Our books might be *Moby Dick, A Farewell to Arms, Cannery Row,* to mention a few. I would eat the ice cream slowly to prolong the story, as well as that special time with my dad and the night. Our secret nights continued for years and years until my teens when books gave way to boyfriends, then college, marriage and babies. But the late night hours still held their magic.

I hadn't realized until recently how all those nights at the kitchen table, dad's music wafting down the hall, the books, and even the ice cream have played such a major role in my life. At my Rimsky-Korsakoffee House in Portland, open now for 33 years, live classical music is performed each night and what do we serve? Just coffee and dessert, mostly ice cream. Then there's the manifestation of my other dream, the Sylvia Beach Hotel, an escape for booklovers on the Oregon Coast. And yes, the rooms are named after authors including Hemingway, Melville, and Steinbeck—to mention a few.

My happiest moments remain late at night, listening to a Brahms intermezzo, sharing ice cream with a coffee house customer, sharing a book with a hotel guest, always remaining grateful for the nocturnal guidance of my loving dad.

After my dad died (in 1990) my dear friend, the journalist and author John Nance, would always join me on the landing at the coffee house with a bowl of ice cream and two spoons. That somehow eased the painful grief I felt in losing my dad.

GOODY CABLE,
PROPRIETOR OF THE SYLVIA BEACH HOTEL AND
RIMSKY-KORSAKOV CAFÉ

I realize that I've spent the majority of my professional musical life not in a conservatory practice room or sun-drenched grand salon but working in cellar cafés; those storefronts where one walks down a series of steps into half-lit spaces where the distance between the bandstand and the audience makes touching one another feel predestined.

In these dim juke joints of the world, peoples' physical actions become long and sharp. From my piano stool, humanity's brooding and complicated movements appear as if they've stumbled out of a Romare Bearden work. They exhibit themselves through slivers of light being cast from cigarettes, clinking bar glasses, even bangles worn by those who are slow dancing—all brought together for the sake of the music and somehow spirit-filled. These cellar cafés can feel like a sanctuary in its better moments.

Nothing ever appears overly planned in these intimate spaces. When the collage of dark and illumination, the music and intention fuse, a flicker of humanity and the thirst to know more ignites— all of us enjoying the bit of light we're casting without exactly praying.

My first professional gigs happened at Cobb's Corner, a Bar located in the Cass Corridor, a stone's throw from Wayne State University and embedded firmly in Detroit's red-light district. Cobb's Corner was considered inner city; located on the corner of Cass and Willis and home to poets, political pundits, Rainbow Party meetings, Detroit Artists' Workshops, college activists, the occasional prostitute, pusher, pimp and many a gregarious local alcoholic. I had a late night "hit" with my quartet immediately following local legend Faruq Z. Bey and Griot Galaxy's set and people were still milling about eager to hear more space music with soul. I had waited eons for this moment and simply couldn't disappoint. It was an unusually cold fall evening, so chilly that even some members of the band has joined many of the bar's patrons and were wearing gloves.

The music that washed over me that night must have splashed on some of the patrons because I remember the pinball machines and pool table falling silent as the set progressed. The place heated up fast. In between tunes and energetic applause came a commotion from the front door. In whooshed saxophonist Pharoah Sanders, in stride with his shepherd's stick and wearing a brocaded African dashiki, who was appearing at the famous Baker's Keyboard Lounge off Livernois and Six Mile Road. He must have been coming to Motown's "new jazz corner of the world" to catch Mr. Bey's group.

Instead, he found an upstart hammering away on a battered upright. We all knew Mr. Sanders's pedigree, his first name bestowed to him by Sun Ra. There was so much energy the moment he entered, I half expected hearing the *Adhan*, the Muslim call to prayer, being recited. Instead of showing his displeasure and simply walking out, he seated himself, nodded approvingly at the music being made, and remained until the set was completed.

I walked out of the bar that crisp morning up in the air not about my future in music, but aware that, like the song says, "The Creator Has a Master Plan."

Christopher Bakriges,
American musician, composer

MILES OF COUNTRY ROADS

The first time I really paid attention to music was when I used to listen to a radio show called "Harlem Rhythms." I was about seven or eight. The show used to come on at fifteen minutes to nine every day, so I was late to school a lot because I was listening to that program. But I had to hear that show, man, had to. Most of the time they played black bands, but sometimes when they had a white band on I would cut it off, unless the musician was Harry James or Bobby Hackett. But that program was really great. It had all them great black bands on there and I remember being fascinated by hearing the records of Louis Armstrong, Jimmie Lunceford, Lionel Hampton, Count Basie, Bessie Smith, Duke Ellington, and a whole bunch of other bad motherfuckers on that program. Then when I was nine or ten I started taking some private music lessons.

But before the lessons, I also remember how the music used to sound down there in Arkansas, when I was visiting my grandfather, especially at the Saturday night church. Man, that shit was a motherfucker. I guess I was about six or seven. We'd be walking on these dark country roads at night and all of a sudden this music would seem to come out of nowhere, out of them spooky-looking trees that everybody said ghosts lived in. Anyway, we'd be on the side of the road—whoever I was with, one of my uncles or my cousin James—and I remember somebody would be playing a guitar the way B. B. King plays. And I remember a man and a woman singing and talking about getting *down!*

Shit, that music was something, especially that woman singing. But I think that kind of stuff stayed with me, you know what I mean? That *kind* of sound in music, that blues, church, back-road funk kind of thing, that southern, Midwestern, rural sound and rhythm. I think it started getting into my blood on them spook-filled Arkansas back-roads after dark when the owls came out hooting. So when I started taking music lessons I might have already had some idea of what I wanted my music to sound like.

Music is a funny thing when you really come to think about it. Because it's hard to pinpoint where it all began for me. But I think some of it had to have started on that Arkansas road and some on that "Harlem Rhythms" radio show. When I got into music I went all the way into music; I didn't have no time after that for nothing else.

MILES DAVIS, AMERICAN JAZZ MUSICIAN, 1926–1991

Sitting on the train to Den Haag
Waiting on the whistle to blow
Amsterdam is fading
But I'm really not ready to go
The ones who came before me
I see them everywhere
By the old canal we were walking
I knew I had been there

Her eyes are like a fire
That burns this night away
The moon is just a liar
The sun will have to say

I left my books and my papers
By the window above the street
The light was shining bright then
I felt like I could leave
And where the gypsy soul goes
God dances and God sings
The stories that will be told
And all the hope we bring

Her eyes are like a fire
That burns this night away
The moon is just a liar
The sun will have to say

But now the dark reflection
By the window where shadows leap
And so life passes by us
Like waking in a dream
Goodnight my sweet lover
Wherever you may be
I'll keep this watch upon us
Though you are far away

Her eyes are like a fire
That burns this night away
The moon is just a liar
The sun will have to say

RB Morris, American writer, musician, and actor

NIGHT PAINTING

I lift three brushes wet with paint. Each brush holds its own hue—ultramarine blue, glowing amber, and a cool black. Airborne Toxic Event's "Sometime Around Midnight" plays on headphones tethered to my iPhone. The room spins like the song. I almost dance as each brush moves across the linen. Wet paint slurred into wet paint. I search for the light in the dark in a painterly chase through the night.

I paint in a refurbished airplane hangar, the night glowing darkly through the skylights above me. Alone in a vast space, my thoughts travel back to years of painting at night: from a loft in SoHo during New York's *Bright Lights Big City* years, to a small makeshift space in Tokyo, to a studio in a reconfigured office building on a block of San Francisco's Market Street that Edward Hopper would have appreciated, to now in a building at an airfield where a fake town was suspended over sensitive areas of the field during WWII to mislead a possible aerial attack.

Like camouflage draped across an airfield, night changes the way we see. Distance is obscured. Color shifts. We see blue tinged black and white under the stars. At night, humans and most vertebrate animals are colorblind because the most sensitive light receptors in our eyes, called rods, detect only black and white. But geckos are different. Painting in what was a military airbase, especially as my mind drifts in the quiet of the night, I often think of the pet gecko my father had in his quarters while stationed in Okinawa. As I struggle to truly see,

I wonder what colors my dad's gecko saw. Geckos evolved from crea-
tures that were active only during daylight, so they did not have rods
for night vision. Over time, through evolutionary adaptation, as geckos
shifted to night-time activity the color receptors in their eyes became
more sensitive and enabled full-hued night vision.

Over the years, perhaps with geckos in mind, I have honed my ability
to see subtle nuances of color both during the day and at night. I collect
moments in my memory by standing still and taking in the sensations
of an evocative evening or a cool dawn. I often begin a painting with
the intention of capturing one of these remembered moments and its
particular atmosphere of color and light. Before I paint, I lay my colors
out on the palette in a range from light to dark and warm to cool. As I
mix my paints, I think about light. I want an interior light that emerges
from the painting. Painting night reveals the contrast between light
and shadow in my artwork and emphasizes the luminosity within the
painting.

My recent oil on linen work "The Azure Hour" combines a certain
sense of beach light and air with the dreams and memories of the urban
night. On evenings in Southern California when the cool ocean breezes
bring a blue fog into the night, it sometimes seems that anything is
possible. The painting took over a year of work to finish. It progressed
in a series of layers, scumbles, and deletions that created an evocation
of the complex nightscape in my mind. I find it necessary at times to
paint at night under subtle illumination to see if the effect that I am
reaching for has begun to take hold. When the light is too bright it

is difficult to see the range of tones from dark to light in a painting. The darkness itself helps create the light. One cannot exist without the other.

Recently, I stood outside in a clearing of a Monterey, California forest near the coast in the middle of the night with my brother and René Boitelle, a painting conservator at the Van Gogh Museum in Amsterdam. Unlike the skies in Los Angeles, we were able to see the stars in the night sky and of course thought of Vincent Van Gogh's painterly evocations of the glittering night. Van Gogh was able to capture the night in his paintings with his skillful use of midnight blue and starry yellow. Gazing at a Van Gogh painting of a star-filled sky, it seems as if he knew that the lights he saw in the dark night had traveled from the deepest reaches of time. According to physicists, as we gaze at the stars, in essence we are looking back toward the beginning of time.

Later that week, I stood with René and another conservator, Devi Ormond, before a Van Gogh painting of a weaver; the painting was laid out like a patient on a table in the Getty Museum's conservation lab. The work seemed so fragile, yet at the same time sturdy and time-less, hearkening back to an era of firelight, candlelight, and moonlight. Soon after Van Gogh painted his weavers, the advent of electricity would completely alter the character of the night. Perhaps in every painting of the night there is a hint of this loss, echoing the shadowed forms in the artwork. I am reminded of the nights many years ago when, before painting, I would put Miles Davis on the record player. I would drop the needle on the first track and listen to the hiss and crackle as *'Round Midnight* began to play—the music always muted, blurred as if it emerged from a smoke-filled room.

Early in my career, as an exhibition of my paintings closed at a gallery in Osaka, Japan, a fellow artist turned to me and somewhat derisively asked, "So what's next? Will you travel from city to city painting their nights?" I didn't come up with a quick rejoinder then. But I know what I would say now: "You can't paint the day without the night."

GREGG CHADWICK, CONTEMPORARY AMERICAN ARTIST

You can live a lifetime and, at the end of it, know more about other people than you know about yourself. You learn to watch other people, but you never watch yourself because you strive against loneliness. If you read a book, or shuffle a deck of cards, or care for a dog, you are avoiding yourself. The abhorrence of loneliness is as natural as wanting to live at all. If it were otherwise, men would never have bothered to make an alphabet, nor to have fashioned words out of what were only animal sounds, nor to have crossed continents—each man to see what the other looked like.

Being alone in an aeroplane for even so short a time as a night and a day, irrevocably alone, with nothing to observe but your instruments and your own hands in semi-darkness, nothing to contemplate but the size of your small courage, nothing to wonder about but the beliefs, the faces, and the hopes rooted in your mind—such an experience can be as startling as the first awareness of a stranger walking by your side at night. You are the stranger.

It is dark already and I am over the south of Ireland. There the lights of Cork and the lights are wet; they are drenched in Irish rain, and I am above them and dry. I am above them and the plane roars in a sobbing world, but it imparts no sadness to me. I feel the security of solitude, the exhilaration of escape. So long as I can see the lights and imagine the people walking under them, I feel selfishly triumphant, as if I have eluded care and left even the small sorrow of rain in other hands.

It is a little over an hour now since I left Abingdon. England, Wales, and the Irish Sea are behind me like so much time used up. On a long flight distance and time are the same. But there had been a moment when Time stopped—and Distance too. It was the moment I lifted the blue-and-silver gull from the aerodrome, the moment the photographers aimed their cameras, the moment I felt the craft refuse its burden and strain toward the earth in sullen rebellion, only to listen at last to the persuasion of stick and elevators, the dogmatic argument of blueprints that said she *had* to fly because the figures proved it.

So she had flown, and once airborne, once she had yielded to the sophistry of a draughtsman's board, she had said, "There: I have lifted the weight. Now, where are we bound?"—and the question had frightened me.

"We are bound for a place thirty-six hundred miles from here—two thousand miles of it unbroken ocean. Most of the way it will be night. We are flying west with the night."

BERYL MARKHAM,
AMERICAN AVIATOR AND WRITER, 1902–1986

At the edge of Honfleur is an impressionist holy site on a plane with La Fournaise and La Grenouillère. La Ferme Saint-Siméon was where Boudin taught Monet about portable easels. Over the years, everyone spent some time there, painting light and trying their luck with the servant girl. Rosie. It was cheap and family style, with lumpy beds and a sumptuous table. Like most of the old spots, it had fallen on hard times. Over the past fifteen years, however, a family of innkeepers had brought it to glory.

I knew I was in trouble when I saw the crowd. The more informally dressed men wore bright ties with their dark suits. A guard dog sat sipping champagne on a plush couch, one of those nonproductive, nondecorative women who let you know the world was created specifically for them. She observed my boat clothes and was not pleased. But this woman had no official status. The hostess and owner was charming.

The large dining room was polished to a glare. Every flower had had its legs waxed. In the lounge, a burnished black piano played itself, and I had no trouble recognizing the tune: "*tum*-ta-tum, *tum*-ta-tum, *tum*-ta-ta-ta-tum. M-I-C-K-E-Y, M-O-U-S-E." Under my shoes, I felt a slight tremor. It could be Eugène Boudin back-flipping to his grave.

My taste buds screamed for lobster, but nearly a hundred bucks seemed a bit excessive. I'm not miserly, I rationalized: I'll be in New England soon and should try something Connecticut can't offer. That turned out to be *bar*, a delicate white fish, in a crispy sesame-tinged crust.

It was delicious. I found a Sancerre that would not disrupt my mortgage payments and relaxed. What the hell. If some people can afford this stuff all the time, who said life was fair? An early Monet Honfleur ain't cheap, either.

I walked outside, planning to stroll around in search of a last image to match that picture in my mind of a wonderful old man offering me the first waters of the Seine cupped in his hands. The moon mugged me. I mean, this was a moon, so huge and round it looked like an exaggerated stage prop, and it was the color of a blood orange. I watched until it was no longer startling, just an unbelievably lovely source of light that splashed gold over the estuary. Its human face seemed animated, but this was no man. I swear to God, Sequana* was talking to me.

MORT ROSENBLUM, AMERICAN JOURNALIST.

[* goddess of the Seine]

DRINKING ALONE BY MOONLIGHT

A cup of wine under the flowering trees;
I drink alone, for no friend is near.
Raising my cup I beckon the bright moon,
For he, with my shadow, will make three men.
The moon, alas, is no drinker of wine;
Listless, my shadow creeps about at my side.
Yet with the moon as my friend and the shadow as slave,
I must make merry before the Spring is spent.
To the songs I sing the moon flickers her beams,
In the dance I weave my shadow tangles and breaks.
While we were sober, three shared the fun;
Now we are drunk, each goes his way.
May we long share our odd, inanimate feast,
And meet at last on the Cloudy River of the sky.

LI PO, CHINESE POET, 701–762
TRANSLATED FROM THE CHINESE BY ARTHUR WALEY

BEDROCK MORTAR FULL MOON ILLUMINATION

Seeing the reflection of the full moon
   in the rainfilled bedrock mortar holes
      where earliest California Indians
   ground acorns with circular grinding stones
And sensing how the full moon
   is like a mortar stone in the sky,
And then seeing the image of my face
   looking up at me from the moonlit surface
and sensing my own evanescence,
   how my face is like an acorn
      time grinds to fine dust,
And thinking thousands of years
   Indians ground acorns here
Singing their acorn songs
   gossiping and laughing
      or silent and musing
   listening to the pleasing sound
      of mortar stones grinding acorns
Or after a big storm
   gazing in the rainfilled holes
      at their reflections
   or seeing the full moon mirrored
Or deer hot from play

dipping shy twilight muzzles
in the cool pools
As blue oak and black oak
ponderosa pine and digger pine
incense cedar and manzanita
grew and died in continuous
ever-changing spots
around the site.
Yet just as surely years from now
faces staring here
After scooping out fallen leaves
and feeling with future fingers
the wet smooth tapering holes
in the mossy lichen-covered rock
contemplating themselves
looking up at themselves
contemplating these same thoughts
will vanish,
While century after century the full moon
continues to stare down
and see its face
unseen by anyone in the forest
Reflected in the rainfilled mortar holes
from long ago.

Antler, American poet

ZORBA'S FIRE

I walked along the edge of the water to say farewell to this deserted shore, to engrave it upon my mind and before going away. I had felt many joys on this beach. My life with Zorba had expanded my heart's realm and some of his words had brought serenity to my mind, but giving simple solutions to the complicated concerns inside me. This human being with his infallible inner spirit, with and his eagle-like primitive glance offered reliable short cuts, reaching, without toil, the peak of effort—attained the unattainable....

While going down a slope Zorba tripped on a stone, which went rolling downhill.

He stopped in amazement, as if he were seeing an astonishing spectacle for the first time in his life. He turned toward me, and in his glance I saw a slight fright.

"Boss, did you see that?" he said after a while. "On slopes stones come alive!"

I didn't say anything, but I felt a deep joy inside me. This is how great visionaries, how great poets see everything—as if for the first time, I thought. Every morning they see a new world before their eyes; they do not see a new world—they create it.

The universe for Zorba, as for the early humans on Earth, was a splendidly rich vision: the stars touched him, the seawaves crashed on his temples. He lived the soil, water, fire, animals, and God, without the distorting interference of reason.

In the moonlight I looked at Zorba and admired the flair and simplicity with which he adapted himself to the world, the way his body and soul became one harmonious entity, and all things—women, bread, mind, sleep—blended instantly and mirthfully with his flesh and became Zorba. I had never seen such an amicable accord between a human being and the universe.

Nikos Kazantzakis, Greek novelist, 1883–1957
Translated from the Greek by Thanasis Maskaleris

Do trains still moan, running away to somewhere in the American dark? They do, clicking and clacking through little, dark, fly-specked towns with never-never names, calling their lonely lament into the night: "Comewithme, comewithme, come...."

"Once we boarded the train to Estonia in the middle of the night.... Inside I fell asleep to the mechanical heartbeat under my ear....You can complain about the drafts and the sheets with stains as old as the Kremlin, but once your head hits that pillow, the train song reaches for you." Oksana Marafioti wrote that in *American Gypsy* (2012).

Trains sing a siren song, as do ships at sea, aircraft no longer earthbound; even as did the old family flivver when we were young and succumbed to sleep in the back seat while the stars winked down. "Now no one can get me," it says. "I leave no tracks. I am alone and this planet belongs to me."

Sight dominates our other senses by day, but when night creeps up, as at the ends of earth, or falls like a stage curtain at the equator, we hear wails of eternal winds across the plains of Wyoming or the Siberian steppes; we smell perfumes of eucalyptus in Australia and orange blossoms in Spain; we feel the softness of talcum powder sands in New Caledonia and the sharp scrapes of Vulcan's stones on the slopes of Mt. Etna; we taste again a Sri Lankan curry so corrosive it made our knees weak.

Once, stroking across the pitch-black sky above the Dark Continent in an Emirates cocoon, I detoured into a fourth dimension. Speed and time vanished in that cozy universe beyond city lights. Far below, the earth fell silent. It was like scuba diving in a dry ocean. In imagination, I pushed the replay button so the trip would not end.

Night life: It's at home aboard the night train from Paris to Istanbul, on the unknown Amazon, along the antique Nile where much of mankind may have been born, up Norway's Arctic coast where children are carried away into the Northern Lights.

So the world spins: No wanderer wants to stop it. We don't want to get off.

GEORGIA HESSE, AMERICAN VAGABOND

NIGHT GAME

It was the game many players called the most exciting they ever played in. And for the fans who saw it or heard Harry Heilmann's broadcast that sultry summer night, it was the most thrilling game ever played in Briggs Stadium. The date was June 23, 1950. The Tigers were in a race with the Yanks that would go down to the wire. Detroit sought to repeat the 5-year cycle that brought pennants in 1935, 1940 and 1945.

More than 51,000 packed the venerable stadium at the corner of Michigan and Trumbull where virtually every major league ball game in Detroit had been played since 1896. But this one was under the lights, still very much a novelty in the Motor City—the first night game in Detroit had been a mere two years earlier.

All day long fans from Wyandotte to Ishpeming talked about two things only: could the Tigers protect their narrow one-game lead over the Yankees and how much would the weather affect the game. Baseballs had a way of flying out of the Stadium when it was hot with high humidity—and that was precisely the forecast for game time.

Former Yankee third baseman Red Rolfe had led the Tigers into first place ahead of Casey Stengel's defending World Champion New Yorkers. Tens of thousands of fans couldn't get tickets, so they huddled by radios tuned to baseball throughout the state to listen to Harry Heilmann—Tigers batting champion in the 1920s—call the play by play. No one would get much sleep that night.

Before it was over, the Yankees would hit four home runs in the first four innings. They would get a late-inning two-run pinch hit home run. And New York pitchers would shut out the Tigers in seven of the nine innings. In all, the Bronx Bombers would crash six home runs. On a normal night, that should be plenty enough to win and move into first place.

The Yanks unleashed their vaunted power early, with four home runs, including shots by Yogi Berra and Jerry Coleman and two round-trippers by Hank Bauer in the first four innings to drive out Teddy Gray and take a 6–0 lead. Shut out through three, the Tigers exploded in the fourth as Gerry Priddy and Walter (Hoot) Evers hit solo shots and Vic Wertz blasted a two-run blow off the rightfield roof. But the biggest belt was struck by relief pitcher Paul (Dizzy) Trout who poled a grand slam. The Tigers seized an 8–6 lead.

But the Yankees weren't through on this record-breaking night.

Joe DiMaggio homered in the seventh. Then pinch-hitter extraordinaire Tommy Heinrich reached the seats with a two-run clout for a 9–8 Yankee lead. Trout, driven from the game, stomped off the field and left the park, furious he had blown the Tigers' valiant comeback.

When Wertz doubled to center in the ninth, that brought Hoot Evers to the plate. Evers's deep drive caromed off the 415-foot sign in right center and the fleet outfielder flew around third and headed for home. He beat Billy Martin's tardy relay to the plate. The inside-the-park four-bagger gave Evers two homers for the night and climaxed the stirring 10–9 double comeback Tigers victory. It was a win in a rare relief appearance for Fred Hutchinson.

Out on Michigan Avenue, Dizzy Trout had stopped his car when he heard announcer Heilmann describe the winning rally. Trout, still in his uniform, danced in the streets, ignoring the traffic jam he had caused. Under the lights of Briggs Stadium, jubilant Tigers fans milled around, unwilling to leave. They had seen a game in which all the runs—19 of them—were scored on home runs. They had witnessed a record-setting 11 home runs, six by New York. And they had seen the Tigers come back—not once, but twice.

There were thrills in the future. A 31-win season for Denny McLain. A World Series championship in 1968 after a season full of comeback wins. The wire-to-wire 1984 championship season ignited by a record 35–5 start. League championships and MVPs in 2011 and 2012. But Tigers fans at Briggs Stadium that electric night of June 23, 1950—and those tuned to Harry Heilmann's broadcast—would forever claim they were on hand for a night game that turned out to be *the* game for the ages.

BILL HANEY,
AMERICAN BASEBALL HISTORIAN, AUTHOR, AND PUBLISHER

PITCH DARK

One night, late in '48, the Tigers are playing
the Senators at old Griffith Stadium.
The game unfolds languorously
until the seventh inning when the Tigers pitcher
goes into his wind-up. He rears back,
kicks high and—
the ballpark lights flicker,
flash, and sputter out—
leaving the field
pitch-dark.
The batter flinches.
The catcher flails.
The umpire lurches.
The infielders and outfielders flop to the ground,
covering their baseball capped heads with raggedy leather mitts.
The fans in the stands strain to hear the familiar crack of the bat,
But hear only the sizzle of surging electricity in the light towers.

Five freeze-framed seconds later
the towers of light blink back on
revealing the nine fielders, the batter, and the umpire,
lying flat on the field,
eyes clenched shut,

hiding from the one play
they'd never practiced.

The only player still standing is the wide-eyed pitcher
Whose arm is frozen in midair.
Looking like an old-time baseball card.

He alone knows
he never
threw
the
ball.

PHIL COUSINEAU

HARES AT PLAY

The birds are gone to bed the cows are still
And sheep lie panting on each old molehill
And underneath the willow's grey-green bough
Like toil a-resting lies the fallow plough
The timid hares throw daylights fears away
On the lane road to dust and dance and play
Then dabble in the grain by nought deterred
To lick the dew-fall from the barley's beard
Then out they start again and round the hill
Like happy thoughts—dance—squat—and loiter still
Till milking maidens in the early morn
Jingle their yokes and start them in the corn
Through well-known beaten paths each nimbling hare
Starts quick as fear—and seeks its hidden lair

JOHN CLARE, ENGLISH POET, 1793–186

THE NIGHT CRY OF THE PEACOCK

The peacock does most of his serious strutting in the spring and summer when he has a full tail to do it with. Usually he begins shortly after breakfast, struts for several hours, desists in the heat of the day, and begins again in the late afternoon. Each cock has a favorite station where he performs every day in the hope of attracting some passing hen, but if I have found anyone indifferent to the peacock's display, besides the telephone lineman, it is the peahen. She seldom casts an eye at it. The cock, his tail raised in a shimmering arch around him, will turn this way and that, and with his clay-colored wing feathers touching the ground, will dance forward and backward, his neck curved, his beak parted, his eyes glittering. Meanwhile the hen goes about her business, diligently searching the ground as if any bug in the grass were of more importance than the unfurled map of the universe which floats nearby.

Some people have the notion that only the cock spreads his tail and that he does it only when the hen is present. This is not so. A peafowl only a few hours hatched will raise what tail he has—it will be about the size of a thumbnail—and will strut and turn and back and bow exactly as if he were three years old and had some reason to be doing it. The hens will raise their tails when they see an object on the ground which alarms them, or sometimes when they have nothing better to do and the air is brisk. Brisk air goes at once to the peafowl's head and inclines him be sportive. A group of birds will dance together, or four or five will chase one another around a bush or tree. Sometimes one will chase himself, end his frenzy with a spirited leap into the air, and then stalk off as if he had never been involved in the spectacle.

Frequently the cock combines the lifting of his tail with the raising of his voice. He appears to receive through his feet some shock from the center of the earth, which travels upward through him and is released: *Eee-ooo-ii! Ieee-ool-ii!* To the melancholy this sound is melancholy, and to the hysterical it is hysterical. To me it has always sounded like a cheer for an invisible parade.

The hen is not given to these outbursts. She makes a noise like a mule's bray—*heehaw, heehaw, aa-aawww*—and makes it only when necessary. In the fall and winter, peafowl are usually silent unless some racket disturbs them; but in the spring and summer, at short intervals during the day and night, the cock, lowering his neck and throwing back his head, will give out with seven or eight screams in succession as if this message were the one on earth which needed most urgently to be heard.

At night these calls take on a minor key and the air for miles around is charged with them. It has been a long time since I let my first peafowl out at dusk to roost in the cedar trees behind the house. Now fifteen or twenty still roost there; but the original old cock from Eustis, Florida, stations himself on top of the barn, the bird who lost his foot in the mowing machine sits on a flat shed near the horse stall, there are others in the trees by the pond, several in the oaks at the side of the house, and one that cannot be dissuaded from roosting on the water tower.

From all these stations calls and answers echo through the night. The peacock perhaps has violent dreams. Often he wakes and screams "Help! Help!" and then from the pond and the barn and the trees around the house a chorus of adjuration begins:

Lee-yon lee-yon,
Mee-yon mee-yon!
Eee-e-yoy eee-e-yoy!
Eee-e-yoy eee-e-yoy!

The restless sleeper may wonder if he wakes or dreams.

FLANNERY O'CONNOR, AMERICAN WRITER, 1929–1964

WHEN MOCKINGBIRD FIRST HEARD ROCK: MIMUS AND THE POLYGLOTTOS

When Mockingbird first heard rock
He cocked his head and crapped
What in hell is that?
It sounded like a train wreck
Someone was screaming
Someone's banging on garbage cans
Mockingbird swooped down
Between the chains of the porch
Swing and swung by the backdoor
And out the other side causing the cat
To jump and knock over a flower pot
He stopped dead still in a Carolina pine
As a guitar solo sailed over
The rumbling clang of a fast moving
Train through a Georgia night
It was raining but it wasn't raining
Mockingbird couldn't figure it out
Some kind of train?
Some kind of big tractor?
Some hurricane or flood?
Some kind of disaster was happening
(But what and where?)

Mockingbird turned his x-ray sonar radar
On the garage door that hung ajar
There were people in there
All yelling and jumping around
Like they was walking on hot coals
Of fire, said Mockingbird
He was reminded of the holy rollers
Handling their big worms
On Sunday mornings
But this was different
This was bigger

This was Saturday night
And it was so loud the moon
Stuck his head in a cloud
Mockingbird couldn't hear his
Voice for the noise
But he hung around
He was spellbound
Something in the sound
Was speaking to him
His blood pounded and rolled
To the mighty locomotion

Mockingbird stayed until the final crash

Until they packed it in and drove away
They've left the building, said Mockingbird

Mockingbird didn't go home that night
He flew downtown
He found some friends
They raved about the sound
Word got around
Others had heard
They started making that sound
They started layin' it down
The news got out
There's good rockin' tonight
And if that Mockingbird won't sing
I know a bird that can do that thing
Sang Mockingbird
He and his mates got with it
They were working the late shift
Bouncing sounds off every wall
All the poles and corner signs
Manhole covers and warehouse doors
The courthouse bell the city clock

They were rockin' round the block
It was intoxicating work

Yeah he was singing the blues
But he was loving it too
The usual birds were all shook up
Reviews were in the ditch/pit
But old MB was having a ball
Mixing it up with the mighty chiefs
He swore he'd never quit
High O Silver! sang Mockingbird
Yeah Yeah Yeah
I can't stop loving you, he (said)
I can't slow down
I can't help myself, he went on
I'm Cathy's clown
I'm all tore up
I'm all tore down
It's her town now, said Mockingbird
Let's get out of this place

Mockingbird and his mates
Blew out of the city gates
They flew the coop
They busted out
For the high and wide
For the high and lonesome
And every low place between

Like a wheel on fire / Just him, a few chickadees
And the boys / And all for the love
Of that joyful noise

RB Morris, American writer, musician, and actor

WALKING WALDEN

This is a delicious evening, when the whole body is one sense, and imbibes delight through every pore. I go and come with a strange liberty in Nature, a part of herself. As I walk along the stony shore of the pond in my shirt-sleeves, though it is cool as well as cloudy and windy, and I see nothing special to attract me, all the elements are unusually congenial to me. The bullfrogs trump to usher in the night, and the note of the whip-poor-will is borne on the rippling wind from over the water. Sympathy with the fluttering alder and poplar leaves almost takes away my breath; yet, like the lake, my serenity is rippled but not ruffled. These small waves raised by the evening wind are as remote from storm as the smooth reflecting surface. Though it is now dark, the wind still blows and roars in the wood, the waves still dash, and some creatures lull the rest with their notes. The repose is never complete. The wildest animals do not repose, but seek their prey now; the fox, and skunk, and rabbit, now roam the fields and woods without fear. They are Nature's watchmen—links which connect the days of animated life.

HENRY DAVID THOREAU,
AMERICAN WRITER, PHILOSOPHER, ABOLITIONIST,
ENVIRONMENTALIST, 1817–1862

WANDERING AT NIGHT

I wander all night in my vision,
Stepping with light feet, swiftly and noise-
    lessly stepping and stopping,
Bending with open eyes over the shut eyes of
    sleepers,
Wandering and confused, lost to myself, ill-
    assorted, contradictory,
Pausing, gazing, bending, and stopping.

How solemn they look there, stretched and still!
How quiet they breathe, the little children in their
    cradles!

The wretched features of ennuyés, the white
    features of corpses, the livid faces of drunk-
    ards, the sick-gray faces of onanists,
The gashed bodies on battle-fields, the insane in
    their strong-doored rooms, the sacred idiots,
The new-born emerging from gates, and the dying
    emerging from gates,
The night pervades them and infolds them.

WALT WHITMAN, AMERICAN POET, 1819–1892

Autumn fades into winter in the fog
and we curtain out the cold at bedtime,
people keep their dogs indoors more,
and the wind in the streets is cold.

Dark days go by and at night
even the stars look different;
we think ahead to turkey dinners
and our plans to celebrate the season.

Death constantly comes closer
and the seasons change and remind us
we won't always give banquets
or all night from our high windows watch
the City sleep and feel the winter come.

JAMES NORWOOD PRATT,
AMERICAN WRITER, POET, WINE AND TEA MAVEN

I once wrote a bestseller in one night, in a dream. It was May twentieth, 1978, the night before the publication party of my first book. Even though I was keyed up for the party I fell asleep easily. The book came to me sometime in the middle of the night. It was original and clever. I felt it contained an important message, maybe even one that would change the world. I knew it would be a hit if it were ever published. I woke up purposefully from my dream, turned over on my side and scribbled the name of the book in pen on a piece of paper. The title was so intriguing I figured it was all I needed to remember the whole story. I eagerly went back to the world of sleep and dreams.

When I woke in the morning I remembered I had an amazing dream about an amazing book, but I had no memory of any details. Then I saw the words I wrote:

Elastic Midnight

I stared at the words for a long time, fascinated. Great title! But what was the story? I didn't have a clue and I finally crawled out of bed and went about my life. But I couldn't get the title out of my head. I became obsessed trying to find the lost story. Finally, I concluded it had something to do with time. The word midnight was a clue.

Midnight is that magical moment when today becomes the past, and tomorrow becomes the now. It's a discrete moment in time, but a fleeting moment gone in a blink. Could the word *elastic* imply I found a way to open up that instant between the now and then? Open it enough to create a passage? And if so, where did the passage lead? What exactly happens in the moment between moments? Is this a place where we can remember the future? I felt like I was close to the story, but also very far away.

My obsession with time took me down different paths. I explored all night celebrations—*Mardi Gras*, Midsummer, *Día de los Muertos*, New Years—seeing them as culturally sanctified times when normal wake/sleep patterns are shattered along with concepts of linear time. Cultural rituals such as these often endure because there are many positive benefits associated with them. I uncovered fascinating research that showed sleep deprivation, prudently applied, can have beneficial effects on depression and some other mental disorders.

Years have passed since my dream, and I feel I never quite got the story right. Still, I know the story in my dream exists out there, somewhere. Does it run around looking for its title like a chicken looking for its head? Is it also obsessed? Who knows, one night, maybe, the story and title will reach across the thin membrane that separates waking and sleeping and be united. It will all be in a good night's work.

MIKKEL AALAND,
NORWEGIAN-AMERICAN PHOTOGRAPHER

The amber lights flicker past as we slip across the long stretch of the Golden Gate Bridge. The twin towers loom above us like colossal sentinels. Foghorns moan and moan across the bay.

Jan stares mournfully at the *neon redly twinkle* of the *white city of San Francisco on her eleven mystic hills,* as her father described it on the long roll of butcher paper that became the notorious runaway novel.

I tell her how much I was moved by her story at Gerry Nicosia's dinner party about the first time she read her father's work. Through the haze of her fourth dialysis treatment of the day, she had described how she was twelve years old and in the hospital for a drinking problem. Her doctor noticed the name "Kerouac" on her medical chart. On a hunch, he asked if she was related to the famous writer. She shrugged. He asked if she'd read any of his books. Petulantly, she shook her head no. A few minutes later, he returned with a copy of *On the Road,* which he handed to her and said, "Read it. It might help."

She told us all this with a tang of regret. "I was up all night," she'd said with end-of-the-world weariness. "By the time I finished I finally understood why my father was never around while I was growing up."

As we pass under the mighty towers of the bridge, I confess to her that I didn't get around to reading it until I was twenty-two. I was languishing in London, working for a professor of literature who thought I needed a jolt to get me, well, on the road again. He climbed the Victorian library ladder in his reading room and pulled down a leather-bound edition of *Seven Pillars of Wisdom* by T.E. Lawrence, a history of the English Secret Service, and a first edition of Kerouac's *On the Road.*

"Your Dad's book was a kind of hurricane for me," I reveal to her. I plunge ahead into No Man's Land, trying to convey the way I felt when all those wind-blown words and bebopping rhythms helped catapult me around the world. Emboldened, I tell her how his *holy goof zany lunacy words* helped catapult me around the world.

A wry smile crosses her face. "Everyone remembers the first time they read that one," she says with sudden childlike exuberance. Her eyes flash with momentary delight, then she asks, "But where are they *now*?" Implying, when his daughter could use some help.

Jan's fingers drum nervously on the window molding of the car door. She seems ravaged by the mean mix of health and literary problems, the struggle to finish her third novel, *Parrot Fever,* and the bitter fight over her father's literary estate. She looks as if she's longing for the quiet anonymity of her motel room.

Slowly, her attention drifts away. She gazes out at the silver wake left by a ship far out at sea. Her sad face is cast in an eerie silhouette that slowly shape-shifts into the spitting image of her father.

For one phantasmagorical moment he's leaning back in the passenger seat of my knockabout '82 Mustang, all peripatetic, poetic, and beat, to paraphrase the playwright. It's Jack ever-lovin' Kerouac, slick and slack in his brown leather jacket, the original coolhunter, wistful in his world of hurt, caught in some dharma bum time-warp between love affairs, tumbledown motels, ramshackle bars, and the long loping backroads, as he wrote, of *bluer than eternity Wildamerica.*

In this *one crazy Roman candle* instant he's staring across the dark bay, longing for the loony locomotion of the open road, digging the long blues line of the distant lowing foghorn on Alcatraz, marveling at the glorious memories of driving his holy goof buddy, Neil Cassady, in an old juddering jalopy under a night-gliding moon, past *groves of lonesome redwood trees*, over boundless plains and beyond the great lakes, listening for bone-deep cries of jazzmen who just *might raise men's souls to joy.*

All the while they're reading from the bluesy manuscript of night like a couple of Zen drunk monks, maddashing into the heart of strange roads at the crackling of the blue dawn.

Go moan, go moan for man, go moan, I hear in the jeweled weirdness.

And now Jan's smoky voice lures me back from my reverie. "So I guess my father wasn't around because he was roaring back and forth across the country, driving like a madman, then sitting in a dark room for months writing about it. He didn't seem to have time for anything or anybody else. Even me. When I figured that out, I was finally able to forgive him."

I ask if she has any other memories of him. With disarming shyness she says, "I remember him coming into my room when I was a little girl and whispering '*Shush*' to my little sisters so he wouldn't wake me.

But that's all, except for one other short visit when I was in my teens."

"It's not much," she concludes with a dash of her father's *doom-tragic* inflection. "But I'll take whatever I can get."

I downshift for the tollbooth and root around in my vest pocket for some change.

"I'm so tired," she says with his *end of the continent sadness*. Her voice is stretched on the rack of night. "I'm so tired of being sick. I don't expect to be around forever, you know."

Her voice catches in her throat, as it did earlier in the night at Nicosia's, when she told us what happened the time she made the pilgrimage to her father's last home, in Florida, in 1994. At first she was frail and vulnerable in the telling, but she gained strength as she revealed how she felt "at home." After serving tea, the new owner, a relative of Jack's last wife, asked if he could get her anything else. In her inimitable way she said exactly what was on her mind. She said she'd love to have her father's rolltop desk.

The response was mocking.

"That's the way the cookie crumbles, Jan."

She was crushed. She owned nothing of her father's.

Listening, it seemed to me that she'd come to live by her father's *go moan for man* words as if they were a mad prophecy.

We pass like phantoms through the toll booth and drive on through the mist shrouding the Presidio, past the darkly floating boats of the Marina. Once again, Jack's words float back to me, summoned by the force of his daughter's inconsolable loneliness: *Happiness consists in realizing that it all is a great strange dream.*

When we reach the Holiday Inn on the Wharf I drop her off, promising to look her up someday in Albuquerque. Jan nods, grievously, then vanishes into the *motel, motel, motel loneliness*, one more cursed child of the famous and legendary. As she hesitantly closes the door behind her, I imagine *locomotives wailing all night long.*

I want to say something to her through the window: *Go on, press on, regardless, everything depends on those who go on.* But I let her go, silently, remembering her old man's nearly last words:

But, no matter, anyway, the road is life....

PHIL COUSINEAU,
SAN FRANCISCO, JUNE 1995

I WALK THE CITY AT NIGHT

I walk the city at night, like the wind,
Like rain. Can you get to sleep by doing this?

Intellect looks to place things in context.
Do not expect that from me.

MEVLANA RUMI, PERSIAN POET AND MYSTIC, 1207–1273
TRANSLATED FROM THE PERSIAN BY COLEMAN BARKS

Coleman Barks's Commentary

Say wandering the city at night is the night-intelligence,
To be contrasted with the mind-intellect, reason,
That which wants to make sense and put things in context.

Walking the city at night is a fine practice.
My friend, John Seawright, used to be a devotee of it.
It is not just a young man's restless way.
I see old men out walking late.

I fly and fly, across the largest ocean in the world, over ice floes or trop-
ical islands, far from any season I know, and get out in an airport that
dissolves all sense of time and place. Long corridors, panels of glass,
screens above every door, clicking over. Men in suits disappearing
down this escalator, appearing from that one, drifting away along that
moving ramp.

I walk and walk as if across a screen myself, and at another gate,
more men in black waiting to disappear into a hole, a stranger comes up
to me and says, "Excuse me. Are you Pico Iyer?" I don't know what to
say, but the safest answer seems yes, and he places a book of poems in
my hands, stands beside me as a flashbulb pops, and then is gone again.

We go up into the sky once more—six miles above the earth now,
and darkness everywhere—and when we descend, a few hours later,
the pilot welcomes us to Ninoy Aquino International Airport, named
after the opposition leader who was killed on this very tarmac not
long before. The night is very dark, and my body, up now for twenty-
five hours—or forty, by my watch—is full of life, ready to walk out
into the morning.

I get into a car and we drive down Roxas Boulevard, sudden fire-
works of silent lights around the gaudy discos and the karaoke parlors,
and then the dark returning all around. I put my things in a hotel and
go out again, with a new-day briskness, to get my bearings in this
foreign place. Men appear in front of me talking about this girl, that

club. Music thumps out of a darkened doorway. Faces are peering out at me as the door opens, and as I take shelter in a beer garden (2:00 a.m. now for the people around me, eleven in the morning for me), I see rats scuttling under the chairs where young girls, alone, eyes closed, are singing last year's love songs.

I get up and walk, to ground myself, to try to imprint on my floating mind something solid and substantial, and as I do I pass a young girl, sitting up abruptly on the sidewalk, and starting to pass a comb through her long, straight hair. She couldn't be more than twelve or thirteen, and yet she gets herself ready for bed as if in a Manhattan duplex, and then lies down again, on the street, and pulls a sheet of cellophane above her.

Around her, all around, whole families are sleeping. Children are huddled on the main divider of the street, and parents, who look as if they expected a future not so different from mine, are stretched out in careful patterns beside the streaking taxis. I walk among these outstretched figures in the dark and another woman smiles out at me from the bushes. She is very young, and very pretty. She says how warm it is tonight, and lonely. She smiles at me in the dark.

I walk and walk, to try to get back what I knew this morning (or was it last night? Two days ago?), but whatever I thought I knew has been effaced, by everything around me. In the casino on the main drag—3:00 a.m. now—there are so many bodies I can hardly move, the lights from the chandeliers catching the excited faces as figures press and shout above the spinning wheel. I step out and go exploring in the beauty salon next door, climbing the grand staircase of an old colonial mansion, and finding, at the top, girls recumbent in the hair-cutting chairs, too poor, I assume, to have real homes in which to sleep. In one room, no less mysterious, a Japanese boy lying flat out on a treatment table, a young woman coming in now and then to adjust the sheet above him, beneath which his feet protrude.

On the street again, by the cloud-covered ocean, the first fathers and their children are beginning to extend their rods into the water as the sun comes up and the traffic begins to intensify behind them. In the grand hotel down the road, which remembers Marcos and MacArthur, sweepers are making the halls immaculate and uniformed workers pass through the dining-room like ghosts. The first elderly couples are out now in the park, whole clusters of them, skittering, and flashing their bright skirts like tropical birds as they practice ballroom dancing.

I go back to my hotel, ready for a good night's sleep—it's coming on for 9:00 a.m.—and when I awaken again, it's dark, the traffic beginning to subside outside my window, the roar of the vacuum cleaners outside my door long gone. The streets are beginning to empty out as I go out into the dark, the men, the women, beginning to congregate in the shadows.

But everything is less strange now because I know the routine in some way, half expect that whisper behind the trees. Very soon I won't make out the people sleeping in the streets. Very soon the shock of the poverty will have become part of the daylight world for me, something I could take for granted.

Pico Iyer, British essayist, novelist, and wanderer

If the library in the morning suggests a severe and reasonably wistful order of the world, the library at night seems to rejoice in the world's essential, joyful muddle.... At night, here in the library, the ghosts have voices.... And yet, the library at night is not for every reader. Michel de Montaigne, for instance, disagreed with my gloomy preference. His library (he spoke of *librairie*, not *bibliothèque,* since the use of these words was just beginning to change in the vertiginous sixteenth century) was housed on the third floor of his tower, in an ancient storage space. "I spent there most of the days of my life and most of the hours of the day; I am never there at night," he confessed. At night Montaigne slept, since he believed that the body suffered enough during the day for the sake of the reading mind....

The various qualities of my readings seem to permeate my every muscle, so that, when I finally decide to turn off the light, I carry into my sleep the voices and the movements of the book I've just closed. I've learned from long experience that if I want to write on a certain subject in the morning, my reading on that subject at night will feed my dreams not only with the arguments but with the actual events of the story....

During the night, I sit and read, and watch the rows of books tempting me again to establish connections between neighbors, to invent common histories for them, to associate one recalled snippet with another....

At the end of the fifteenth century, to exercise his memory among the books he knew best, Niccolò Machiavelli preferred to read in his study at night—the time when he found it easiest to enjoy those qualities which for him most defined the relationship of a reader and his books: intimacy and leisured thought. "When evening comes," he wrote, "I return home and go into my study. On the threshold I strip off my muddy, sweaty, workday clothes, and put on the robes of court and palace, and in this graver dress I enter the antique courts of the ancients and am welcomed by them, and there I taste the food that alone is mine, for which I was born. There I make bold to speak to them and ask the motives for their actions, and they, in their humanity, reply to me. And for the course of four hours I forget the world, remember no vexations, fear poverty no more, tremble no more at death: I pass into their world."

Like Machiavelli, I often sit among my books at night. While I prefer to write in the morning, at night I enjoy reading in the thick silence, when triangles of light from the reading lamps split my library shelves in two. Above, the high rows of books vanish into darkness; below sits the privileged section of the illuminated titles. This arbitrary division, which grants certain books a glowing presence and relegates others to the shadows is superseded by another order, which owes its existence merely to what I can remember. My library has no catalogue; having placed the books on the shelves myself, I generally know their position by recalling the library's layout, and areas of light or darkness make little difference to my exploring. The remembered order follows a pattern in my mind, the shape and division of the library, rather as a stargazer connects in narrative patterns the pinpoints of the stars; but the library in turn reflects the configuration of my mind, its distant astrologer. The deliberate yet random order of the selves, the choice of subject matters, the intimate history of each book's survival, the traces of certain times and certain places left between the pages, all point to a particular reader. A keen observer might be able to tell who I am from a tattered copy of the poems of Blas de Otero, the number of volumes by Robert Louis Stevenson, the large section devoted to detective stories, the minuscule section devoted to literary theory, the fact that there is much Plato and very little Aristotle on my shelves. Every library is autobiographical....

ALBERTO MANGUEL, CANADIAN WRITER, TRANSLATOR, ANTHOLOGIST

LAST NIGHT, ALONE

Last night, alone with a wise elder, I said,
Please. Do not hold back from telling me
any secrets about this universe.

Leaning near, he spoke into my ear,
Some things cannot be told
or understood, only seen
and lived wisdom.

MEVLANA RUMI, PERSIAN POET AND MYSTIC, 1207–1273
TRANSLATED FROM THE PERSIAN BY COLEMAN BARKS

Coleman Barks's Commentary:

Bawa used to talk about the *taste* of what he knew.
In the Preface to Book II of the *Masnavi*
Rumi quotes the Arab saying,
He who does not taste, does not know.

PART III

A HARD DAY'S NIGHT

In a real dark night of the soul, it is always three o'clock in the morning, day after day.

— F. SCOTT FITZGERALD

L egend has it that when the Beatles emerged from Abbey Road Studios, in London, after a marathon recording session for their first movie, drummer Ringo Starr turned to John Lennon and said, "It's been a hard day..."—then looked around and noticing that it was still dark outside—added the word "night." What Lennon heard was one continuous phrase—"hard day's night," which he later called another "Ringo-ism." The phrase was as percussive as Starr's drumming technique, perfectly capturing the rigors and tensions of working hard through the night. Paul McCartney later said that he and Lennon immediately knew they had the name of the title track and the movie itself. Lennon claimed that he turned the phrase into the first verse of the song: "It's been a hard day's night and I've been working like a dog..." and completed the song within twenty minutes. When their fans heard the title and lyrics they immediately understood its meaning, a tough but meaningful and productive night of work, even if you know you "should be sleeping like a log."

For some, like the Beatles, night is a blessing, inspiring poems, movies, songs, inventions, political revolutions, love affairs. For others, like poet Dylan Thomas or essayist May Sarton, it's a haunting, a source of fear or pain, a stretch of hours to be endured like a toothache. Night is no longer friend, but foe. The dark powers that once inspired now conspire. "Ain't it just like the night," moans the old blues singer, "to play tricks when you're trying to be quiet?" Unquiet, we can't work. Our dreams are transmogrified, rife with monsters and insecurities. Hope disintegrates into despair; faith corrodes into cynicism. What liberates one person suffocates another, a feeling that was mythologized many generations ago when it was believed that the oppressive feeling in our chest during a restless night of sleep was caused by something grim sitting on it. The *grimoires* of the time groaned with spells to fight off the monster variously called a nighthag, a *cauchemar*, "the fiend that tramples," and a wild horse, a demented mare, which in turn sired our word *nightmare*, which is the nemesis of this sleepstrange part of the night journey.

Out of the sheer cussedness of insomniac nights come the melancholic, anguished words of those who find the darkness to be a torture chamber, the bed a rack, and sleep a canvas of Magritte phantoms.

The selections in Part III mark this still point of the night journey. Our nightwriters include the poets Abu Amir ibn al-Hammarah, Zi Ye, Yang-ti, and Ovid, who aptly describe the paralysis of insomnia, and Samuel Taylor Coleridge, who describes his depression as "The Seems" as in "what seems to be & is not—men & faces & I do not [know] what."

For lovers like Ovid, during sleepless nights "cruel love torments the breast." The tumultuous-hearted James Joyce finds "a riot of emotions" as he sleeps next to his wife. These cameos about creative responses to sleep deprivation anticipate several writers in this part. "Night Rain," by Izumi Shikibu, is a triumph of creative melancholy or healing wistfulness over the curse of insomnia, which was rampant in the imperial courts of Kyoto a thousand years ago.

In the early eighteenth century a certain Count Goldberg, the slumberless Russian ambassador to Germany, approached the greatest composer of the era with a curious commission. The count was stricken with insomnia, and he asked Johann Sebastian Bach to provide a musical cure for his sleeplessness. Bach's *Goldberg Variations* were the melodic result. There's no telling what kind of beauty might be wrestled from the beast of night.

If the insomnolent ambassador, or anyone else, had gone to Lewis Carroll, a century later, for a cure for their insomnia, they would have been given a set of math problems, "calculations," from Carroll's *Bedside Book*, which the fantasist regarded as remedies for the "harassing thoughts that are apt to invade a wholly-unoccupied mind."

Finally, for those not convinced by the slumbersome Anthony Burgess that there is no cure for nocturnal horrors except not going to bed, there is movie therapy. *The Cure for Insomnia* is not the life story of Goldberg, the Russian ambassador, nor the name of a snake oil salesman's brochure. Instead, it's the title of the longest film on record, a strategically soporific eighty-seven-hour-long documentary.

Similarly, any crack lets light through, as Leonard Cohen sang, and that is how the light comes through. It is that light that provides the dark clarity of the night world, which has the uncanny capacity to heal us. Night heals in the way the soul is tempered, one degree, one battle at a time—the way consciousness is built, through steady struggles with forces older and greater than ourselves. What the contributors in this book have in common is that they have wrestled with what D.H. Lawrence called the "gruesomes," savaging depression. Still, he was able to write in the "Song of a Man Who Has Come Through": "What is the knocking at the door in the night? / It is somebody who wants to do us harm. / No, no, it is the three strange angels. / Admit them. Admit them."

Say no more; some of us come from rusted nights.

INSOMNIA

When the bird of sleep
thought to nest
in my eye

it saw the eyelashes
and flew away
for fear of nets.

Abu Amir ibn al-Hammarah,
Andalusian poet, 12th century
Translated by Cola Franzen from the Spanish versions of Emilio
Garcia Gomez

I HAVE BROUGHT MY PILLOW

I have brought my pillow and am lying at the
northern window,
So come to me and play with me awhile.
With so much quarreling and so few kisses
How long do you think our love can last?

ZI YE (LADY MIDNIGHT),
CHINESE POET, 265-320
TRANSLATED FROM THE CHINESE BY ARTHUR WALEY

ALL NIGHT I COULD NOT SLEEP

All night l could not sleep
Because of the moonlight on my bed
I kept on hearing a voice calling:
Out of Nowhere. Nothing answered, "yes."

ZI YE (LADY MIDNIGHT),
CHINESE POET, 265-320
TRANSLATED FROM CHINESE BY ARTHUR WALEY

WINTER NIGHT

My bed is so empty that I keep on waking up:
As the cold increases, the night-wind begins to blow.
It rustles the curtains, making a noise like the sea:
Oh that those were waves which could carry me back
    to you!

YANG-TI, 605–617
TRANSLATED FROM THE CHINESE BY ARTHUR WALEY

UNTOUCHED BY SLEEP

What shall I say this means, that my couch seems so hard the cover-
lets will not stay in place, and I pass the long, long night untouched
by sleep, and the weary bones of my body are filled with ache?—for
I should know, I think, were I in any way assailed by love. Or can it
be that love has stolen into me and cunningly works my harm with
covered art? Thus it must be; the subtle darts are planted in my heart,
and cruel love torments the breast where he is lord.

OVID,
ROMAN POET, 43 B.C.E.–17 C.E.
TRANSLATED FROM THE LATIN BY CHRISTOPHER MARLOWE

Oh, the fore shift dark and dreary,
Oh, this lonely two o'clock;
Limbs may ache, and hearts be weary,
Still there comes the caller's knock;
And each blow upon the panels
Bids us up and don our flannels,
By the light of lamp or can'les
Batter at the grimy rock.

Just to get a bare subsistence,
Little earned and nothing saved,
With the workhouse in the distance
After we for years have slaved.
Some look on with holy horror,
At each pitman's little error,
But t'would much abate their terror
Could they see the dangers braved.

To the coal's grim face we travel,
And again our flannels doff;
Can they wonder if we cavil
At the ones much better off?
Like a snake our bodies coiling,

Weary hours of incessant toiling,
Through each pore the sweat comes boiling;
Think on this, ye ones that scoff!

Up while stars are dimply peeping
Through the midnight's sable gloom;
Up while pampered ones are sleeping
In their snug and cosy room.
Fore shift visions need not haunt them,
Nor the pit's grim danger daunt them;
Oh, t'was a kind of fate to plant them
Where they could so safely bloom!

MATTHEW TATE,
ENGLISH POET AND SONGWRITER, 1837–1900

MACHINES SHED ALUMINUM TEARS

How they suffer, the machines—
shift after shift, day after day, year after year.
Their only relief for repair. No wages
but the immortality of replaced parts.
They cannot resolve every night before bed
to give the next morning their two weeks' notice.
They have no beds, no dreams. While I sleep
their eyes are held open by other hands.
Other hands shuffle their tears
in search of defects. Each machine
is a crippled dream of perpetual motion.

Tonight my ears are not the battered coasts of their weeping.
I do not see aluminum sheets drop through the press
like seconds through a guillotine clock,
I do not handle countless cardboard tubes
regarding them as blinded telescopes.
My friend and I have called in sick.
We are in Lake Park deep in the 2nd shift night,
high on breaths of our friendship.
I try to forget the machines, I cannot comfort them.
I cannot give them the rest of rust
or even the dream of it. Tonight

I lie on my back on a picnic table
and the face of my friend gazes down at me
from the deep night sky of stars.

JEFF PONIEWAZ, AMERICAN POET

I can see that in the midst of darkness light persists. Hence I gather that God is Life, Truth, Light. He is Love. He is Supreme Good....

Prayer needs no speech. It is in itself independent of any sensuous effort. I have not the slightest doubt that prayer is an unfailing means of cleansing the heart of passions. But it must be combined with the utmost humility.

As food is necessary for the body prayer is necessary for the soul. Prayer is an impossibility without a living faith in the presence of God within. God demands nothing less than complete self-surrender as the price for the only real freedom that is worth having.

Never own defeat in a sacred cause and make up your minds henceforth that you will be pure and that you will find a response from God. But God never answers the prayers of the arrogant, nor the prayers of those who bargain with Him. If you would ask Him to help you, go to Him in all your nakedness; approach Him without reservations, also without fear or doubts as to how He can help a fallen being like you.

The prayer of even the most impure will be answered. I am telling this out of my personal experience, I have gone through the purgatory,

Prayer is the key of the morning and the bolt of the evening. "It is better in prayer to have a heart without words than words without a heart." [John Bunyan]

I am giving you a bit of my experience and that of my companions when I say that he who had experienced the magic of prayer may do without food for days together but not for a single moment without prayer. For without prayer there is no inward peace.

The more my faith in God increased, the more irresistible became the yearnings for prayer. Life seemed to be dull and vacant without it. In fact food for the body is not so necessary as prayer for the soul.

I have found people who envy my peace. That peace, I tell you, comes from prayer; I am not a man of learning but I humbly claim to be a man of prayer. I am indifferent as to the form. Everyone is a law unto himself in that respect....

After I had practiced [silence] for some time I saw the spiritual value of it. It suddenly flashed across my mill that that was the time when I could best hold communion with God.

Let everyone try and find out that, as a result of daily prayer, he adds something new to his life, something with which nothing can be compared.

Mahatma Gandhi,
Indian spiritual and political leader, 1869–1948

Dinofelis was a cat less agile than a leopard or a cheetah but far more solidly built. It had straight, dagger-like killing teeth, midway in form between a saber-tooth's [tiger], and say, the modern tiger's. Its lower jaw could slam shut; and since, with its slightly cumbersome build, it must have hunted by stealth, it must also have hunted by night.... Its bones have been unearthed from the Transvaal to Ethiopia: that is, the original range of man....

Could it be, one is tempted to ask, that *Dinofelis* was Our Beast? A beast set aside from all the other Avatars of Hell? The Arch-Enemy who stalked us, stealthily and cunningly, wherever we went? But whom, in the end, we got the better of?

Coleridge once jotted in a notebook, "The Prince of Darkness is a Gentleman." What is so beguiling about a specialist predator is the idea of an intimacy with the Beast! For if, originally, there was one particular Beast, would we not want to fascinate him as he fascinated us? Would we not want to charm him, as the angels charmed the lions in Daniel's cell?...

[If we] allow for one big cat, for several cats, or for horrors like the hunting hyena—[we] have reinstated a figure whose presence has grown dimmer and dimmer since the close of the Middle Ages: the Prince of Darkness in all his sinister magnificence.

BRUCE CHATWIN,
ENGLISH WRITER, 1940–1989

DRIVING WITH JACK AT MIDNIGHT

We drove in darkness,
the amber lights of Sonoma
receding in my rearview mirror,
shadows leaping like thieves
from eucalyptus trees
along the night road.

How do you lead a child
into the dark forces of night
and back again?

What can you say to your
squirming son after he watches
soldiers shoot children
on the evening news?

What can you say when he turns your bones blue
by asking you from the backseat of the car,
"Please, Papa, hold my hand.
It's dark all around me."

Dark had never sounded so ominous.
I reach across the back seat, feeling the velvet

darkness on my fingertips, and clasp his
trembling hand in my best tough and tender
grasp, then hear him whisper,
as if to reassure *me*,
"Just until it gets light again, Papa."

Driving one-handed, I listen
for the reassuring sound of his sleep,
remember the moment I held him for the first time,
all crinkled and crying, blinking and trying
to open his gummed-up eyes,
startled by that light
after all that darkness.

Hurtling home past long-abandoned railroad tracks
And farmland lost to grapevines, I spin
The green-glowing dial of the car radio
And hear Springsteen wailing
Like a lost locomotive how he'd
"Drive All Night" to be with
the love of his life,
because he loved her
heart and soul,
heart and soul,
heart and soul.

And hearing that lonesome moan, I sing along
until I feel my dead father's voice vibrating
in my throat, I sing until I hear traces
of my own voice in my son's as he cries,
"Papa, how much longer? How much
longer is it going to be
dark?"

Only then did the words spring free,
the short lie I told to tell the longer truth,
"Don't worry, buddy, we'll be home soon.
I won't let the darkness hurt you."

PHIL COUSINEAU

TAKE THAT RIDE

I don't want to die like Agee
In the back of some taxi on the run
So much time wasted, the feast of life
Just tasted then it's gone
But the life that he was living and the
Gift that he was giving were all one
The bad comes with the good
The madness and love, it's all or none

I don't want to end up like Terry Malloy
In a cab carrying on about how it's gone
How he could have been a contender
And people would remember what he'd done
But there's fights that you don't take
And there's nights when you break and you run
Just do what you can do and answer to who
You have to when you're done

But take that ride
'Cause we fly tomorrow
To the other side
If we make it through tonight
And truth or lie

Beg, steal, or borrow
It will follow
As the road goes out of sight

I don't want to die like Hank Williams
In the back of some rented limousine
Drifting through the night
So far from the light that he had seen

But this road we've been riding
Looks a lot like the road that he was on
A lost and lonesome highway
That some still take to find their way home

RB Morris, American writer, musician, and actor,

No Man's Land (Flanders Fields), First World War, 1914

Karel Lauwers, a peacetime artist and a signaler with the Twelfth Regiment on the outskirts of Oostkerke, nor Diksmuide, recorded in his diary that from his trench, which had "frozen well," he heard the Germans singing "their Christmas songs, and if I had known, I would [have been close enough to] understand." As he bent around an unusual open fire, as no shots were being fired, "the wet mist was covering our backs and heels and the whole field as with a white layer." When daylight came he would do a charcoal sketch of huddled soldiers.

German gestures of peace became contagious, although no one forgot the war. Hugo Klemm of the 133rd Saxon Infantry Regiment recalled being assembled before church in the village of Pont Rouge, in which they billeted, to be warned by the company commander that they had to be on the alert on moving into the line. The English might exploit Christmas. Yet his company had already secured two trees, which, with candles lit, they mounted above their parapets. The Saxons also laid fresh planks on the muddy footpaths of the trenches before settling in to celebrate as best they could. Just in case, once darkness set in, Klemm wrote, "We fired the occasional shot from our outposts to let the enemy know we would not let ourselves be surprised."

Both to his left and to his right Klemm watched candles being lighted on trees fronting other Saxon trenches. Latecomers were the reserve company of the 133rd led by Lieutenant Johannes Niemann, which had celebrated in advance. Aware that they were to move into the trenches on Christmas Eve, Niemann's men had opened their *Llebesgaben* in their rear area, sharing surplus boxes from home with puzzled villagers. "Then at darkness we marched forward to the trenches like Father Christmas with parcels hanging from us. All was quiet. No shooting. Little snow. We placed a tiny Christmas tree in our dugout—the company commander; myself, the [other] lieutenant, and the two orderlies. We placed a second lighted tree on the parapet. Then we began to sing our old Christmas songs: '*Stille Nacht, heilige Nacht*' and '*O du fröhliche.*'"

Their singing attracted almost as much attention across No Man's Land as did the lighted trees, which an English soldier described as "like the footlights of a theatre." Many units were spellbound, then reacted, as if an audience, with applause. Albert Moren of the Second Queen's Regiment, near La Chapelle d'Armentières, remembered many years later that the "performance" began just after dark. "It was a beautiful moonlit night, frost on the ground, white almost everywhere; and...there was a lot of commotion in the German trenches and then there was those lights—I don't know what they were. And then they sang '*Silent Night*'—'*Stille Nacht.*' I shall never forget it. It was one of the highlights of my life."

From across the barbed wire British units shouted for more, and some Germans replied with "*O Tannenbaum.*" Fired from Very signal pistols, appreciative British flares soared up. Too distant at Fleurbaix to see them, the 2nd Bedfordshires, according to Lieutenant Charles Brewer, then nineteen, were appreciating the fact that "for once it wasn't raining." They could peer out over their top row of "saddened sandbags" and see in the moonlight the trenches and barbed wire "not 100 yards away, across the slimy churned-up morass of No Man's Land. A body or two lay out there. Everything was still, except the occasional tok-a-tok of a machine gun. In my own strip of water-logged trench a chilled sentry stamped and beat his mittened hands. Suddenly he saw a group of glistening lights appear on the German parapet."

"Look out!" he called. "Keep your perishin' heads down. I bet it's a sniper's trap." Brewer was fetched from a dugout to have a look. "I saw that the lights were on a Christmas tree. Farther along the line I could see Christmas trees sparkling." Then his company began to hear, "splendidly sung," what they could recognize as *Stille Nacht.* They gave the Jerries a cheer; then one of Brewer's chaps shouted, "Ere, let's sing 'em something back. Come on!" And they sang, less artistically but no less heartily, "We are Fred Karno's Army," irreverently exploiting the tune of the hymn "The Church's One Foundation."

STANLEY WEINTRAUB.
BRITISH PROFESSOR, HISTORIAN, BIOGRAPHER

NHAC SANH

I seep through a darkness
as thick and wet as hot black soup.
Distant riverboats gurgle. Distant stars prickle.
Out of this liquid midnight
a dog stirs, yaps three times,
then fades back into shadows.

In our bunkhouse old vets sleep.
Nhac Sanh's singing once told them
whether an enemy was near.

Tonight is a silent night, save for their snores
and our single tree locust
screeching, screeching, screeching.

Tonight they are safe to dream.

EDWARD TICK, AMERICAN PSYCHOTHERAPIST AND POET

(Nhac Sanh is a night-singing insect in the cicada family. The size and shape of a large locust, it is found in the Mekong River Delta of Southeast Asia. It was familiar to troops who fought there during the Vietnam War.)

For I am the future ghost
Hiding in another verse now
Still I am wandering about looking for action
Which I have neglected for minutes, months, decades.

Yes, it is myself curious about what I am funding:
The Karsh Chardin in a whirlpool of human faces.
I cannot talk with them. They are busy like Elijah.
Let them go.

I am on my island like Ingmar
Bergman on Faro with his memories on film.

This radio music is what he would choose for sentiment
Just enough for my mood. Just enough.

Now here is a Shadow with a chessboard at midnight.
But I have not the wit for chess nor the desire.
Charlemagne couldn't get the hang of writing
Even with his Alcuin. Rare spirits. Fellows.

This midnight belongs to me. I have the oil.
This is not a dream. This is my shift but

In the morning I will curse this excursion and call it a lie.

GARY YOUNG, AMERICAN POET-PRIEST

THE DANGERS OF READING ALL NIGHT

When old Mr. Lynch reached the top rung of the ladder he saw the book he had been searching for wedged between the towering stack of books he was leaning against and the rafters of his grandmother's roof. The ladder swayed precariously as he stood on his tiptoes to reach for the book. He tugged gently, and as he pulled it out he dislodged a dog-eared copy of Hawthorne's *Twice-Told Tales*, which fell and thumped on the floor far below. He tugged again and watched as a moldy edition of Macaulay's *Lays of Ancient Rome* and a rare volume of *Prehistoric Guernsey* fell from their perches and bounced off the ladder on their way down to the floor of the attic. One last time he pulled, and out flew a copy of *Look* magazine with the fetching photo of Marilyn Monroe on the cover. Foolishly, he lunged for it and nearly toppled over.

Damn, he thought, *I've been looking for that magazine for years.*

Clouds of book dust billowed around him. The ladder swayed dangerously, and he felt a wave of nausea roll through him. Relieved, he steadied himself and held up the book that he had been lusting after for years so he could read the title on the leather binding: *The History of the Decline and Fall of the Roman Empire, Volume VI,* by Edward Gibbon. The gold letters gleamed in the faint light. His heart pounded with anticipation. Over the years he'd read the first three volumes of Gibbon's masterpiece, but then he'd lost track of the final one with the English historian's controversial conclusion. Couldn't find it for the life of him, like so much else in the sprawling mansion.

This is why you never throw anything out, he said to himself. *You never know when you're going to have to know something.*

Mr. Lynch clutched the book in his hand like a long-lost friend. Slowly, he made his way down the ladder, trying not to knock over anything else, which was easier said than done. All around him were towering piles of books, newspapers, magazines, pamphlets, telephone books, old Rudy Vallee LPs, horseracing forms, baseball and football yearbooks, Sears Roebuck catalogs, and car repair manuals. They were haphazardly stacked from floor to ceiling in the shadow-strewn attic. He could hear the cooing of pigeons on the roof above him, the scritching of mice underneath the floorboards below, and his own throat-clutching breathing.

When Mr. Lynch reached the bottom of the ladder he turned his body sideways so he could thread his way through the labyrinth of books to the pull-down stairs that led him back to the main part of the house and his puce-colored overstuffed reading chair.

Standing in the hallway, Mr. Lynch had to catch his breath before navigating his way through the cramped passage into the night-darkened parlor. If he squinted, he could just make out the light from the Tiffany lamp. Here, there, and everywhere were books, books, and more books. They rose from the swaybacked hardwood floors to the flaking plaster rosettes on the ceiling. He sucked in his ample stomach and slithered down the hallway, his face brushing up against the loose-leafed magazines, and yellowed newspapers, and hundreds of read and unread books.

Each unread one felt like a reproach.

Someday I'll make a list, he vowed, *so I can find them when I want them and want them when I find them.*

Sharp slants of light shot across the house, revealing the lost world of books he'd been hoarding since his grandmother died. He glanced around the room and felt a riot of emotion roiling in his heart. It was the thrill of books to remember mixed in with the dread of books already forgotten.

The air was thick with dust, bird droppings, and mold from the thousands of books he'd been hoarding since he was a kid. Somewhere he'd read that he should be careful about mold growing on those old books, but he'd never gotten around to dusting, much less cleaning everything with vinegar and water, which was supposed to be the only solution.

Twenty more yards, he calculated. *I know I can make it.*

With a grunt, he shoved aside several unopened boxes of God-knows-which books. Each box was a reminder of the long walks he'd made all over Oakland and Berkeley, to every library, bookstore, and Salvation Army outlet. Finally, he was able to creep the last few yards into the musty parlor, where his reading chair waited for him, the last gasp of empty space in the boarded-up mansion where he had been hiding for years. Nine square feet of freedom where sat his overstuffed reading chair. Smiling wanly, he changed his old loafers for his threadbare slippers and allowed himself to fall down into the chair.

He never wanted to get up again. Here was his home within a home.

A single blade of amber light slanted in through a hole in the wall next to the front door. That was the tell-tale sign that the street lights in front of the house had flickered on. It was at least nine o'clock. The soft light landed on a pallet full of his grandmother's antiques he couldn't bear to part with. He looked longingly at her old Victrola, the Singer sewing machine, a Detroit Electric stand-up radio, a pallet full of steamer trunks, and books, books, books, and more books. The room was starting to look like one of those barns that sold antiques he'd once seen in West Marin when he was a kid. Maybe he should have a yard sale? He could use the money to buy the 1933 second edition of the Oxford dictionary he'd always wanted. No, then people would want to start poking around inside the house, looking for more books, and this and that. Not worth the trouble.

All I want to do is read, he muttered to himself as he settled down into his trusty reading chair, a puce-colored piece of furniture only a grandmother and a book-hound could love. Mr. Lynch stared at the heavy tome in his hand and quickly calculated the number of chapters he could read before dawn. *Now this is heaven*, he thought. This was what he lived for, the anticipation of a languorous night of reading. Smacking his lips with glee, he cracked open the Gibbon book and began to revel in Rome's slow descent into madness.

Near dawn, the hour of the wolf, *le temps du loup*, as his French-Canadian grandmother used to call it, he was startled by a loud creaking sound. *The house settling in*, he thought, annoyed that his reverie had been broken. Moments later came a muted roar. *Probably another stack of newspapers falling down.*

Out of the corner of his eye, he saw the fifteen-foot-high pile of *National Geographic*s that loomed over him bulge and shift. He considered ratcheting his old bones out of the chair and rearranging them, but his eyes were drawn back to his book by the centripetal force of the story he had been dying to read.

Near dawn, Mr. Lynch awoke from a dream-addled sleep. *The Decline* was open to a passage in Chapter LXIX that he tried to read through bleary eyes: "Vicissitudes of fortune, which spares neither man nor the proudest of his works, which buries empires and cities in a common grave."

A common grave?

Was that where he left off?

Where was I? he wondered. He riffled through a few more pages to Chapter LXXI and read, "All that is human must retrograde if it does not advance." *Ah, yes, I remember now*, he thought, and went promptly back to sleep.

His last thought being, *One chapter to go. Tomorrow, I'll finish up.*
He never knew what hit him.

The first to topple were the *National Geos*, then the six volumes of Proust's *In Search of Lost Time*, then twenty-two books out of the hundred and four that his boyhood hero, Ray Bradbury, had published. Each pile that fell triggered a paper avalanche. A history of paperweights toppled over, followed by an analysis of the drinking habits of the French *voyageurs* in the Yukon. The avalanche continued. A wooden crate marked STROH'S BEER filled with his collection of Topps baseball cards that his mother told him she'd thrown out when he didn't go to the prom in his senior year of high school. When the box hit the arm of Mr. Lynch's reading chair it broke open and out flew hundreds of baseball cards, like magician's doves released from his stovepipe hat.

Strangely, the very woman Mr. Lynch used to refer to as a "Nosy Parker," was the neighbor who smelled something putrid coming from his house and took the time and trouble to call the police. When Officer O'Reilly from the Oakland police department arrived at her house he jotted down a few routine notes and nodded wearily at the ramshackle Victorian mansion next door.

"Okay, I'll check it out, Mrs. Garvey," he said. "Probably just a dead skunk under the house. You did the neighborly thing by calling us."

Stepping onto Mr. Lynch's front porch the officer yelled out his name. No response. He tried to jimmy open the front door, but it wouldn't budge. He found an axe in the truck of his police car and used it to claw an opening large enough to reach the inside handle. When he coaxed it open, the door burst off its hinges and he was knocked off his feet by a deluge of books. He shook his head in disbelief and pushed his way through the door and was flabbergasted to see the mountains of junk. He used the axe to hack his way through it like a tunneling miner, advancing slowly in the direction of the God-awful stench in the center of the parlor.

An hour later, he found Mr. Lynch buried with his nose in a thousand books. One by one, Officer O'Reilly pulled them off the bewhiskered old man. With no little disdain, he tossed aside bestsellers and obscure works, old copies of *Sports Illustrated* and scattered volumes of the *Encyclopedia Britannica*, cartons of *Popular Mechanics* magazines from the 1940s, and a Manhattan phonebook that felt heavy enough to be a wheel stop for a 747.

Five days, more or less, Mr. Lynch had been rotting there, the coroner said later. When the media got a whiff of the story, Mrs. Garvey told the reporter who knocked on her door that the saddest part of the whole sorry episode was that the "old hoarder," as she called him, had never returned all those books and magazines to the libraries where he'd borrowed them.

"Imagine the late fees Mr. Lynch piled up," she added mournfully. "If he paid them our local library could've stayed open. Word on the street is that he just kept telling the librarian he lost the books. She must have felt sorry for him."

The reporter politely asked her if she'd ever been inside her neighbor's house. She said no. Why bother. She couldn't read. They had nothing to talk about.

ROB LaCHANCE, FRENCH-CANADIAN JOURNALIST

THE FIRST QUIET DRINK OF THE EVENING

"I like bars just after they open for the evening. When the air inside is still cool and clean and everything is shiny and the barkeep is giving himself that last look in the mirror to see if his tie is on straight and his hair is smooth. I like the neat bottles on the bar back and the lovely shining glasses and the anticipation. I like to watch the man mix the first one of the evening and put it down on a crisp mat and put the little folded napkin beside it. I like to taste it slowly. The first quiet drink of the evening in a quiet bar—that's wonderful."

I agreed with him.

"Alcohol is like love," he said. "The first kiss is magic, the second is intimate, the third is routine. After that you take the girl's clothes off."

RAYMOND CHANDLER, AMERICAN WRITER, 1888–1959

NOCHE DE LOS MUERTOS

We are pressed, our backs to the wall, in Balmy Alley, a bottleneck of a back street in San Francisco's Mission District, as the dead drift by.

Skeletons on stilts, in bridal gowns, playing drums in steel bands— *los muertos*, the dead—proceed in almost single-file procession through a cramped alleyway that feels like the birth canal to another world.

We are skeletons too. My husband, Lowry, and our friend Jeff are tall, gaunt, black-caped, and spectral. The white markings on the chest of Lowry's black shirt suggest a ribcage. Jeff's black gloves are spidered with bones. Earlier in the evening, at a table in the window of a Yucatan restaurant, I used grease crayons in white, black and red to hollow out eyes and noses and widen grins, painting our faces like skulls as passersby pointed and gawked.

Every year in the Mission, on the heels of Halloween, the Dia de los Muertos Procession, part of a celebration that fuses Aztec beliefs in death and afterlife with the Christian Day of All Saints, sets forth from the corner of 24th and Bryant.... Over 10,000 people crowd the crossroads on the night of this supernatural juncture, and yet the scene is oddly subdued, laced with a potent mix of reverence and expectation.... People flow into the intersection, greetings exchanged in murmurs.... Fingers of incense rise up from the crowd and twirl away into the twilight. Then there is music, Aztec flutes and drums, and the procession sets off at a dreamy shuffle.

Up 25th we amble reflectively—mothers, fathers, children, pets—

and then down 24th, the music, the smoke, the bruisy-blue warmth of an Indian summer eve massaging us into altered states…. Our crowd stretches across the street. We feel powerful and anonymous, magically garbed as the dead. On the corners, the musicians stop to perform.

But it is in Balmy Alley as the parade nears its final destination and the crowd thins, by necessity, to a sly trickle that this otherworldly assembly comes truly alive. Pirates, babies, ingénues, clowns, old men, dancing girls, drummers and dogs shake, rattle and roll their clavicular way down the bemuralled aperture. It is tight and close in the narrow passageway, and warm and suffocatingly intimate, and I have never felt safer than here, in this dimly lit funnel of a street surrounded, as I am, by the dead. We wait, let the circus push past, then follow it, burped back out into the open on 25th between Treat and Harrison Streets at the southern end of Garfield Park.

The park is aglow with candles and altars. The bands set up on the sidewalks around it. Creepily clad celebrants cavort at its corners. A big group gathers at an altar in front of a swing set wrapped in crepe paper and garlanded in flowers where papier-mâché skeletons sitting on swings are caught in eternal frolic. Amid *velas* and pictures and offerings and incense, people crouch, kneel and sit in aspects of meditation and prayer. I wander through the park adrift in the half-light, watch the young, the old, the living, the dead, circle, pause, and salute one another. The smoke of our candles, the light of our flames, the energy of our dreams and hopes and love flare up and out, and the darkness bears down to embrace us. The community of both worlds swings back and forth, back and forth, on the arc of a fearless affection. The dead never leave us; we leave them, not knowing how to entertain spirits, how to keep them at home in our lives. Tonight we remember; we make room for the dead. Tonight, they are among us.

LINDA WATANABE MCFERRIN,
AMERICAN WRITER AND POET

ADVANCING ON THE CHAOS AND THE DARK

Trust thyself: every heart vibrates to that iron string. Accept the place the Divine Providence has found for you, the society of your contemporaries, the connection of events. Great men have always done so, and confided themselves childlike to the genius of their age, betraying their perception that the absolutely trustworthy was seated at their heart, working through their hands, predominating in all their being. And we are now men and must accept in the highest mind the same transcendent destiny; and not minors and invalids in a protected corner, not cowards fleeing before a revolution, but guides, redeemers, and benefactors, obeying the Almighty effort and advancing on Chaos and the Dark.

RALPH WALDO EMERSON,
AMERICAN WRITER, 1803–1882

BURNING THE MIDNIGHT OIL

Burning the midnight oil
and my candle at both ends
in a race to save the planet
from the mega-catastrophe
euphemistically referred to as
Global Warming, I followed
my own fossil footprints
to a coal-burning power plant.

Thoreau was right!
and eco-prophetic as usual:
Awake in time to witness the sunrise.
And after you witness the sunset
don't turn on whale oil lamps
or coal-burning lamps
or river-damming lamps
or nuke-waste-producing lamps.

When night falls, just go to sleep.
And if you awake in the night with an idea
for a poem you just *must* jot down,
light a candle or turn on your trusty
solar-powered mini-flashlight.

JEFF PONIEWAZ, AMERICAN POET

IN A DARK TIME

In a dark time, the eye begins to see,
I meet my shadow in the deepening shade;
I hear my echo in the echoing wood—
A lord of nature weeping to a tree.
I live between the heron and the wren,
Beasts of the hill and serpents of the den.

What's madness but nobility of soul
At odds with circumstance? The day's on fire!
I know the purity of pure despair,
My shadow pinned against a sweating wall.
That place among the rocks—is it a cave,
Or winding path? The edge is what I have.

A steady storm of correspondences!
A night flowing with birds, a ragged moon,
And in broad day the midnight come again!
A man goes far to find out what he is—
Death of the self in a long, tearless night,
All natural shapes blazing unnatural light.

Dark, dark my light, and darker my desire.
My soul, like some heat-maddened summer fly,

Keeps buzzing at the sill. Which I is *I?*
A fallen man, I climb out of my fear.
The mind enters itself, and God the mind,
And one is One, free in the tearing wind.

THEODORE ROETHKE, AMERICAN POET, 1908–1963

DO NOT GO GENTLE INTO THAT GOOD NIGHT

Do not go gentle into that good night,
Old age should burn and rave at close of day;
Rage, rage against the dying of the light.

Though wise men at their end know dark is right,
Because their words had forked no lightning they
Do not go gentle into that good night.

Good men, the last wave by, crying how bright
Their frail deeds might have danced in a green bay,
Rage, rage against the dying of the light.

Wild men who caught and sang the sun in flight,
And learn, too late, they grieved it on its way,

Do not go gentle into that good night.

Grave men, near death, who see with blinding sight
Blind eyes could blaze like meteors and be gay,
Rage, rage against the dying of the light.

And you, my father, there on the sad height,
Curse, bless, me now with your fierce tears, I pray.
Do not go gentle in that good night.
Rage, rage against the dying of the light.

DYLAN THOMAS, WELSH WRITER, 1914–1953

BOURBON

Fireflies, the dark heat,
a deep humidity begins evaporating

and night is dented with this small array of stars
from a motel—*Stardust* or *Star-Lite*,

I can't remember now.
The bones of your body—dear cage

for keeping you.
The way they make your body old

beneath your muscles. Almost ghost
limbs. Trunk of a small car, clicked open, metal

in that slow *plié*. Our fingers grip
the handles of our luggage, pull it from the dark.

Your hands. Your mother,
a whole family

crowds into the room with us.
It's summer. We unpack.

The contents of our suitcases
are mingling…this seems right.

SARAH MACLAY, AMERICAN POET

CHILDHOOD RADIO SIGNAL IN THE ALIEN DETROIT NIGHT

My chin on the cool sill. Green rocking chair sixties pink daisies painted on the arms. Night rocket to the stars with transistor radio, batteries and a slight burning smell. We lived in the same brick house with aluminum frames and different color bricks in the same subdivision; handsome, athletic, fervent you and wavery, dreamy me. I had a flowering crab apple and a rock collection with crystals I could imagine came from the surface of the moon, while the woman next door had poodles, a tan, and décolletage. Your lawn had a lush, convex curve. My father also cleaned up, smelled good. But he never went anywhere—that he wanted to go—with my mother. As if she did not count, could not think, didn't know how to have a good time. I pondered. Maybe Mom really didn't *know* what to do. Did *women* feel, did they know what a good time *was*? Then what could I do if I was to be a woman? If it was inevitable? How could I stop the disintegration of personality, of character, of consciousness, that came with the female body? Stop fecundity? The smell of grass and blood? That was new to me then. Sex seemed key, yet I hardly knew what it was. (Did you? As you ran like an inspired automaton around the track?) If a boy could talk to me through my body, I would still be human, if still a girl. And just maybe, through the portal, the moment, fueled by the magical realism of sex, there would be enough time, enough strength left over to be alive. To do something. To be something. This is what I thought, my window like a windshield deflecting insects at warp speed, riding the night radio, keening frequency, low crackling sound. Gender misting the pavement and dark shrubs like dew. The whole street a big future, haunted mothership to space.

JOYCE JENKINS,
AMERICAN POET AND PUBLISHER

BORGES AND THE DARKNESS VISIBLE

In the light, we read the inventions of others; in the darkness, we invent our own stories. Many times, under my two trees, I have sat with friends and described books that were never written. We have stuffed libraries with tales we never felt compelled to set down on paper. "To imagine the plot of a novel is a happy task," Borges once said. "To actually write is an exaggeration." He enjoyed filling the spaces of the library he could not see with stories he never bothered to write, but for which he sometimes deigned to compose a preface, summary, or review. Even as a young man, he said, the knowledge of his impending blindness had encouraged him in the habit of imagining complex volumes that would never take printed form. Borges had inherited from his father the disease that gradually, implacably weakened his sight, and the doctor had forbidden him to read in dim light. One day, on a train journey, he became so engrossed by a detective novel that he carried on reading, page after page, in the fading dusk. Shortly before his destination, the train entered a tunnel. When it emerged, Borges could no longer see anything except a colored haze, the "darkness visible" that [John] Milton thought was hell. In that darkness Borges lived for the rest of his life, remembering or imagining stories, rebuilding in his mind the National Library of Buenos Aires or his own restricted library at home. In the light of the first half of his life, he wrote and read silently; in the gloom of the second, he dictated and had others read to him.

ALBERTO MANGUEL,
CANADIAN WRITER, TRANSLATOR, ANTHOLOGIST

NIGHT TRAIN HOME

I am in a dark tunnel
in the dark of night
during dark times.

I cannot tell
if my tunnel was made
by God or humans
until street lights,
bridge and house and traffic lights
crackle the treeline
like pond ice.

Then I know that the dark
is older than the walls
we build against it.
Then I see the lights
we hurl like spears of fire at the abyss
falling among our own far-flung troops.

Can't sleep / Still the middle of the night I guess
I'm not looking for a clock
I hear trains clanging over
Rails a mile away

I hear a mockingbird working
The graveyard shift
I wake up and worry
Worry about debts I owe
Things I've left undone
The love I don't give
The regrets, I guess
I wake up and can't go back to sleep
Sometimes I read
But the bedside lamp may wake her too
And she needs her sleep
Before the alarm goes off
So I come in here

I've already got a list of to do's for the day
Fill out a non-custodial parental form
For my daughter's college
Mail books and CDs
Try to do some promotion for this show
On Wednesday
Contact a string of people
About one thing and another
Including Europe
Just a few more shows in Ireland

And we should break even
Stuff like that
I mean, that's the good stuff

But it's nice
Nice to hear the night birds sing
A concert not many take in
And yet encore after encore
Night after night
Nice to feel the quiet
Such as it is
And watch the sky ease itself
Through a prism of changes
Cutting shapes through curtains and blinds
Across ceiling and walls
Like the dreams you left back in bed
Like the people and places you've known
In your life
All your life
Coming to this night

RB MORRIS, AMERICAN WRITER, MUSICIAN, AND ACTOR

So limitless the darkness seems
that I could walk through its wood
and reach each place I missed today
exhausting neither time nor mind.
Night lies like a star-studded die
in my hand and I want to cast
it constantly, desperate to
yet redeem the debts of the day.
But baffled by just half a chance
can't roll seven or eleven.
Night's fixed however I fight it
I always crap out about one,
hating the great addiction—sleep—
despising Morpheus the thief
and my body's nodding weakness.
Collapsed with clothes and light both on
I punish my daily failure
with a troubled, crippled sleep that
now steals hours from tomorrow.

There's a choice beneath the habit:
how to bend to today's cycle,
spin in the sun's course not mine, let

my watch notch the arrow of time.
Day is to be seized, but the night
the night is for surrendering,
a method training us for death—
to let go, surrender the night.

KENT CHADWICK, AMERICAN POET AND TEACHER

WHEN ENCOUNTERING A GHOST FOR THE FIRST TIME

When encountering a ghost for the first time it is necessary to remain as calm as may be and to retain the normal courtesies of civilized society, viz. on meeting a ghost in the street after dark a gentleman should *always* raise a hat. However, should you be lying in bed affeared lest you might meet a ghost, having never met one before, the simplest method of allaying those fears is to conjure up a shadowy ghost of your own.

I dreamt I dwelt in marble halls,
And each damp thing that creeps and crawls
Went wobble-wobble on the walls.

By positioning your hands so as to form certain configurations and by placing your hands between a source of light—be it a moonbeam or a lamp—and a blank wall, you can ensure that what goes wobble-wobble on your bedroom wall is not a fiend but a friend.

CHARLES LUTWIDGE DODGSON (LEWIS CARROLL), ENGLISH WRITER AND
MATHEMATICIAN, 1832–1898

She was fast asleep.

Gabriel, leaning on his elbow, looked for a few moments unresentfully on her tangled hair and half-open mouth, listening to her deep-drawn breath. So she had that romance in her life: a man had died for her sake. It hardly pained him now to think how poor a part he, her husband, had played in her life. He watched her while she slept, as though he and she had never lived together as man and wife. His curious eyes rested long upon her face and on her hair: and, as he thought of what she must have been then, in that time of her first girlish beauty, a strange friendly pity for her entered his soul. He did like to say even to himself that her face was no longer beautiful, but he knew that it was no longer the face for which Michael Furey had braved death.

Perhaps she had not told him all the story. His eyes moved to the chair over which she had thrown some of her clothes. A petticoat string dangled to the floor. One boot stood upright, its limp upper fallen down: the fellow of it lay upon its side. He wondered at his riot of emotions of an hour before. From what had it proceeded? From his aunt's supper, from his own foolish speech, from the wine and dancing, the merry-making when saying good night in the hall, the pleasure of the walk along the river in the snow. Poor Aunt Julia! She, too, would soon be a shade with the shade of Patrick Morkan and his horse. He had caught that haggard look upon her face for a moment when she was singing "Arrayed for the Bridal." Soon, perhaps, he would be sitting him in that same drawing-room, dressed in black, his silk hat on his knees. The blinds would be drawn down and Aunt Kate would be sitting beside him, crying and blowing her nose and telling him how Julia had died. He would cast about in his mind for some words that might console her, and would find only lame and useless ones. Yes, yes: that would happen very soon.

The air of the room chilled his shoulders. He stretched himself cautiously along under the sheets and lay down beside his wife. One by one, they were all becoming shades. Better pass boldly into that other world, in the full glory of some passion, than fade and wither dismally with age. He thought of how she who lay beside him had locked in her heart for so many years that image of her lover's eyes when he had told her that he did not wish to live.

Generous tears filled Gabriel's eyes. He had never felt that himself towards any woman, but he knew that such a feeling must be love. The tears gathered more thickly in his eyes and in the partial darkness he imagined he saw the form of a young man standing under a dripping tree. Other forms were near. His soul had approached that region where dwell the vast hosts of the dead. He was conscious of, but could not apprehend, their wayward and flickering existence. His own identity was fading out into a grey impalpable world: the solid world itself, which these dead had one time reared and lived in, was dissolving and dwindling.

A few light taps upon the pane made him turn to the window. It had begun to snow again. He watched sleepily the flakes, silver and dark, falling obliquely against the lamplight. The time had come for him to set out on his journey westward. Yes, the newspapers were right: snow was general all over Ireland. It was falling on every part of the dark central plain, on the treeless hills, falling softly upon the Bog of Allen and, further westwards, softly falling into the dark mutinous Shannon waves. It was falling, too, upon every part of the lonely churchyard on the hill where Michael Furey lay buried. It lay thickly drifted on the crooked crosses and headstones, on the spears of the little gate, on the barren thorns. His soul swooned slowly as he heard the snow falling faintly through the universe and faintly falling, like the descent of their last end, upon all the living and the dead.

JAMES JOYCE, IRISH WRITER, 1882–1941

THE NIGHT WILL PASS

A night full of talking that hurts,
my worst held-back secrets.
Everything has to do with loving and not loving.
This night will pass.
Then we have work to do.

MEVLANA RUMI, PERSIAN POET AND MYSTIC, 1207–1273
TRANSLATED FROM THE PERSIAN BY COLEMAN BARKS

LYING AWAKE

September 18

...This morning I woke at four and lay awake for an hour or so in a bad state. It is raining again. I got up finally and went about the daily chores, waiting for the sense of doom to lift—and what did it was watering the house plants. Suddenly joy came back because I was feeling a simple need, a living one. Dusting never has this effect (and that may be why I am such a poor housekeeper!), but feeding the cats when they are hungry, giving Punch clean water, makes me suddenly feel calm and happy.

Whatever peace I know rests in the natural world, in feeling myself a part of it, even in a small way.... To go with, not against the elements, an inexhaustible vitality summoned back each day to do the same tasks, to feed the animals, clean out barns and pens, keep that complex world alive.

MAY SARTON, AMERICAN WRITER, 1912–1995

TYMNES

This headstone marks a white Maltese.
All his life they called him Bull.
He guarded Eumelus faithfully.
Now, night's silent roads
Have swallowed up his barking.

Ancient Greek epitaph
Translated by Michael Wolfe,
American filmmaker, poet.

THE NIGHT ROSES

And then I could feel their strange weight, wet as night as they fell
from her hands, even the stems flush with scent and dew—and in the
center of this large bouquet, too large to hold—even the cabbage a too-
large rose, even its leaves now petals—as every daily thing is remem-
bered and fondled as a rose—even the folded night, even the silence of
its singing.

Even its dark song.

Sarah Maclay, American poet

BLACK ROSES

When I was working as a florist at Posey's Flower Shop, in Dearborn, Michigan, back in the 1960s and '70s, a few times a week the phone would ring, always just as the shop was closing. During the summer that meant around eight p.m., but in the dead of winter, especially around the holidays, it could be after midnight. After working such grueling hours, my friend Agnes and I hated to hear that ring because we were desperately tired and dying to go home.

Our tough German boss, Roger, used to cast a cold eye on the wall phone. He would pick up the receiver without even saying hello. He would just hold onto it until the gruff voice came on, which could be heard clear across the flower shop. He would pull a long face and grunt as he wrote down the order. Usually, it was for four dozen roses, but sometimes the voice would demand five or even six dozen. None of us who worked there ever dared ask who was on the other end of the line. We kept our mouths shut. We needed the job.

It was strange, or what have you be. But it wasn't the number of flowers that was unusual. Detroit was flush in those days because the car companies were making money hand over fist. Every day we got huge orders, especially from Ford's World Headquarters, or the Big Glass House, as we all called it, a few miles away, down Michigan Avenue. What was odd about the late-night orders was what we were told to do with the roses.

"I want the *special*," the mystery voice would ask. "The Miller's special."

That was code that Roger had worked out with the mystery caller just in case, my fellow florist Agnes explained to me, someone was bugging the phone. The *special* was black roses. Not the bluish-black roses that some florists claim they've seen. I don't believe them. I've never seen them. The orders were for jet black, death black roses. He was *ordering* us to paint the roses black, petal by petal, hundreds of petals, that had to be painted by hand. Agnes, whom I worked with hand in glove at the long wooden preparation table, used to joke that it wasn't just painstaking work. "It's *paintstaking*, Rosemary," she would say. "It's a pain to paint petals."

But that wasn't the strangest part.

When we finished painting the roses we had to cut off their heads.

The first time Roger brought an order to me I thought it was another one of his bad jokes. At times he showed a gallows sense of humor about life in Detroit. Lots of jokes about dead bodies floating on Lake St. Clair, or why the Rouge River used to catch on fire.

"We need these *right away*," Roger would mutter to me or to Agnes. "They don't want any screw-ups, either."

"*Black* roses?" I shot back, thinking he was making fun of our work. But I could tell that he was deadly serious. He'd had a snootful of threats from our midnight caller. We heard them. The funny thing was that none of us dared ask who was calling or who got the black roses. But you had to be stupid not to know. Innately, we knew what was happening. The calls were coming from the Purple Gang, our Midwest version of the Mafia.

They were a nasty bunch of characters. It was common knowledge that the gang started out during Prohibition as bootleggers and hijackers and brothel owners. By the 1960s they were racketeers who made their money from drugs, gambling, money laundering, and extortion. You name it and they had their filthy mitts on it. They terrified storeowners all over town. One time, Ma confided to me in a *hush-hush* manner that my father had to pay protection money to "those gangsters" every month because they'd threatened to burn the building down.

All this was on my mind whenever I watched Roger out of the corner of my eye when the phone rang after hours. I could tell by the way his face contorted that he hated being their patsy. He was torn in every direction except loose. But innately I knew he didn't have any choice. It wasn't just the fear of God that the gangsters stirred up in him. Those orders were by far his biggest moneymaker.

In those days, the late 1960s, a dozen roses cost the average Joe walking in off the street about twenty-five dollars. But Agnes and I, who were his favorite florists, had to spend a lot of time—which was *overtime* that he dreaded paying—to paint each petal. Those petals were satiny, fragile little things, and they could break off the stem if we weren't careful. So Roger charged the gangsters a hundred dollars for a dozen black roses, which works out to about a thousand dollars in today's money. That was cheap for what we felt was a kind of slave labor, or at least hazard pay, like what those Mohawk Indians got for building the skyscrapers in Manhattan. Agnes used to joke that we were really getting paid a little extra for our silence. Anyway, if you multiply twenty-five bucks by five or six-dozen, you get the idea. Roger was making a small fortune off those guys. As far I know, the hoodlums never balked about the price, so it must have been worth every dollar to them. They paid for perfection and we gave it to them. Perfectly black roses that we painted for them in the perfectly black night, after hours, when no one could see us working.

I'm always asked if I was scared. No, I was no nervous Nellie. To me, the work was a challenge. I've always wanted to be painter. I love flowers. I enjoyed taking the roses, when they were still red, from the walk-in refrigerators where we stored them, and laying them out one by one on the preparation table. I liked opening up each individual rose until it looked like it was in bloom. Then I would take a small-haired paintbrush and coat the petals from top to bottom and on the sides, until it looked like they'd grown that way.

Well, if they had come straight from the tomb.

The worst part was the bit about cutting their heads off. The very idea was disgusting, a little morbid, if you love roses like I do. The heads would *plop* off. That bothered me. I couldn't help thinking about someone placing their heads under a guillotine and having their heads chopped off. It could have been the tricks that the lights played on us after hours. They used to flicker on and off and that gave us the heebie-jeebies. Or it could have been the influence of that dreadful Edgar Allan Poe movie, *The Pit and the Pendulum,* that my husband had forced my kids and me to see at the State Wayne. That weirdo Vincent Price tortured the poor hero by strapping him to a slab of a table while a huge blade slowly swung back and forth until it was an inch from the guy's throat.

"You're always babying them," Stan would snipe. But I was right. The kids had nightmares for a week after seeing it.

But orders were orders.

So I used a sharp pair of shears to sever the heads from the stems and then tie the flowers together with a black band and place them into a cellophane bag. Then I tied the bag with a black satin bow and placed it at the bottom of the box. The interior of the box was lined with black linen paper. I stuck the stems into a small black Styrofoam brick that was soaked in water to keep the flowers fresh. Black, black, black. Sometimes I felt like a mortician. To me, the finished boxes resembled dark coffins, final resting places for my roses.

And then we were told in no uncertain terms to deliver the grim boxes into neighborhoods where angels dare not tread, in the danger zones where Dearborn butted up against Detroit.

If you had half a brain, you knew what the score was. The word from our delivery boys was that our little works of art, the black roses, were being sent to the shadiest bars, the most sordid strip clubs, and the most dangerous chop shops that were like a blight all over the Metro area. But, really, that wasn't so shocking, or what have you be. What *was* shocking was finding out how stupid some men can be. We learned that most of those flowers were going to idiots who were dumb enough to sleep with the girlfriends or wives or sisters of the leaders of the Purple Gang. How stupid can you be? It was those lame-brained lover boys who got the six-dozen black roses orders hand-delivered to them. The threat was clear as mud. If they didn't shape up, they were doomed. They would soon be six feet under, like the local union boss, Jimmy Hoffa. And the world is still looking for him.

Eventually, I got the courage to ask my Italian-American brother-in-law, Andy Lozzi, in Dearborn, if there was some kind of tradition of black roses back in the old country, in Sicily, which his parents had escaped from during the war. With a frown I'll never forget, Andy told me that it was an old Mafia ritual. Black roses were delivered as death threats. And, he said, in no uncertain terms, "Be careful, the tradition came over here on the boats: *'If you don't stop messing around, off with your head.'*"

Suddenly, it all made sense. Knowing that made my job a little less scary. And the other thing that eased my mind was hearing Roger call my brother-in-law's mother, who was head of the Dearborn police department. Roger always called her right after taking the orders from the mob. "Okay, Sergeant McCann, I got another one of *those* orders," he would mutter. Within minutes we would hear the police sirens. That meant she'd dispatched her best "spotters," officers in squad cars who worked the hot spots, the high crime areas, where the black roses were always directed.

Agnes was scared to death, but I never worried about it. I knew if we kept our mouths shut and didn't say boo we would be fine.

Eventually, Roger would get a message back from the gangsters that the flowers had been delivered. I recall him slipping up one time when he arrived early at the shop after a late night delivery. He just gave me a sly thumbs-up, which I took to mean, "That loser out on Miller Road got the message."

Thirty years later, I still wonder why my boss trusted me with such dangerous work. There I was, working for one of the meanest and most vindictive gangs in the country and I didn't bat an eye. All I can think of is that he wasn't afraid of much because he was born on the streets of Detroit, and then there was the protection that my brother-in-law's mother gave us. I like to think he also believed I was scrappy and kind of fearless. Working with the dreaded Purple Gang didn't scare the crap out of me. We had a few willynillies working there, older women who complained. I thought they were fragile teacups. Me, I was never scared about what might happen when I was in the flower shop. It's not like they were going to raid us with Mrs. McCann keeping an eye on the place. I have to admit there were nights that I looked in my rearview mirror as I drove home.

Eventually, the little ritual with the black roses came to an end because we couldn't find any more drivers. They kept quitting on us because it was too dangerous. My favorite driver was Ernie Rogowski. One night, in the middle of the horrendous Christmas rush, he came back from a delivery into the projects. He was swearing like a long-shoreman. As he punched out his time card, he muttered to me that he'd rather not live the rest of his days worrying about getting shot for delivering some stupid flowers. "Purple Gang or no Purple Gang," he said defiantly, throwing down the keys to the delivery truck.

Long past midnight, on Christmas Eve, 1968, when we all should have been home with our families, the phone rang. My heart sank like the elevator down at J. L. Hudson. I was desperate to get home. I couldn't hear what Roger was saying but could see he was angry. For years he had been taking their guff and their orders because he thought the shop needed the money. That night was different. He looked relieved, as if he was no longer afraid of retaliation. His spine was stiff with determination. As he passed by me at the wrapping table, he mumbled, "It's too damned nerve-wracking anymore."

My first thought was *Oh, twiddlepaddle. I'm going to miss the black roses.*

I always wanted to be a painter.

ROSEMARY LACHANCE,
FRENCH-CANADIAN FLORIST AND PAINTER

PART IV

THE DREAM FACTORY

"To sleep, perchance to Dream;
Aye, there's the rub...."

— WILLIAM SHAKESPEARE,
HAMLET

O verhead glides the moon. The earth rumbles below. The question for lovers of the night, as the band Mumford & Sons call them, is: "To bed, perhaps to sleep? To sleep, perchance to dream? To dream, possibly to wake, to rest and maybe finish our work tomorrow?"

The desire for sleep is strong, as the Roman writer Martial wrote, because it "makes darkness brief," as is the desire to make it last as long as possible, which Irish storytellers call "eating the darkness," as if digesting it replenishes us in some strange way.

The oneiric state of the long night's journey is full of ambiguity. It might be amorous, rife with longing, as Homer knew when he described the "sweet sleep" that lured Odysseus home into the arms of Penelope after their twenty-year travail—sleep "that loosens the limbs of men... loosening the cares of the soul." But it is also anxiety-ridden, giving rise to such thoughts as the Elizabethan description of going to sleep as being "buried in bed," a sepulchral thought embodied by Shakespeare's Macbeth, who speaks of sleep as the death of each day's life, or Keats as the "soft closer of our eyes," or Anthony Burgess as the "gentle rocking travel along the river of the dark."

How timeless the connection between night, sleep, and love, as we go further on down the road of night. The sixth-century Greek philosopher Pythagoras could have been writing yesterday when he described our tentative moments of dozing as the time for "daily action to be scanned." The indefatigable Leonardo believed in the advantage of "finding oneself in bed the dark to go over again in the imagination's eye the ideas of the day." An extract from Thomas De Quincey's book about the last days of Immanuel Kant, the nightly ritual of the "self-involved" philosopher who swathed himself in quilts "like a mummy" so he might be inspired. "Looking at Them Asleep," by Sharon Olds, is an exquisitely observed poem that gently captures the held-breath silence that hovers when we watch our children slumber.

The midnight riders here have found ways to hold fast during those fractious hours just before dawn. The Old Man of the Mountain, Lao Tzu, recommended contemplating the stars; the Benedictine monk Brother David Steindl-Rast encourages practicing gratefulness.

It is there when we have the eyes to read the black ink on the dark paper of night, the time when "darkness is visible," as William Styron described his struggle with depression. For Styron there was a dark luster to the consolation he felt in reading the ending of *The Divine Comedy*. Only after Dante had forged his way through the dark wood and harrowed hell with his mentor, Virgil, could he write:

E quindi uscimmo a riveder le stelle.

And so we came forth, and once again beheld the stars.

I fell asleep thinking of him,
And he came to me.
If I had known it was only a dream
I would never have awakened.

ONO NO KOMACHI, JAPANESE POET, 834–880
TRANSLATED FROM THE JAPANESE BY KENNETH REXROTH

CHANG TZU'S DREAM
(THE DREAM OF THE BUTTERFLY)
梦 MENG

Once upon a time,
Zhuang Zhou dreamt he was a butterfly,
fluttering hither and thither,
blissfully content in being a winged creature;
hence, the butterfly was utterly unaware of Zhou's existence.
Upon abrupt awakening, he was somewhat startled and befuddled
to find that he was Zhou.
Ah! Is Zhou a butterfly in the dreamscape,
or is the butterfly dreaming of being Zhou?
However, Zhou and the butterfly
must each have their own distinct being.
Accordingly, this is what is called
the metamorphic transmutation,
Wu Hua.

ZHUANG ZHOU (CHANG TSU),
CHINESE PHILOSOPHER, 389–286 B.C.E.
TRANSLATED BY SAT HON WITH ALICIA FOX

A DREAM OF MOUNTAINEERING

A night, in my dream, I stoutly climbed a mountain,
Going out alone with my staff of holly-wood.
A thousand crags, a hundred hundred valleys—
In my dream-journey none were unexplored
And all the while my feet never grew tired
And my step was as strong as in my young days.
Can it be that when the mind travels backward
The body also returns to its old state?
And can it be, as between body and soul,
That the body may languish, while the soul is still strong?
Soul and body—both are vanities:
Dreaming and waking—both alike unreal.
In the day my feet are palsied and tottering;
In the night my steps go striding over the hills.
As day and night are divided in equal parts—
Between the two, I *get* as much as I *lose*.

Po Chu-i, 772–846
Translated from Chinese by Arthur Waley

LET NOT SLEEP COME UPON THINE EYES

Let sleep not come upon thy languid eyes
Before each daily action thou hast scanned;
What's done amiss, what done, what left undone
From first to last examine all, and then
Blame what is wrong, in what is right rejoice.

ATTRIBUTED TO PYTHAGORAS, 570–495 B.C.E.
TRANSLATOR UNKNOWN

THE BENEFITS OF THE DARK

I have proved in my own case that it's of no small benefit on finding oneself in bed in the dark to go over again in the imagination the main outlines of the forms previously studied, or of other noteworthy speculations; and this exercise is entirely to be recommended, and it is useful in fixing things in the memory.

LEONARDO DA VINCI,
ITALIAN PAINTER, INVENTOR, 1452–1519
TRANSLATOR UNKNOWN.

GOLDEN SLUMBERS

Golden slumbers kiss your eyes,
Smiles awake you when you rise:
Sleep, pretty wantons, do not cry,
And I will sing a lullaby:
Rock them, rock them, lullaby.

THOMAS DEKKER, ENGLISH WRITER, 1572–1632

Those who don't feel this Love
pulling them like a river,
those who don't drink dawn
like a cup of spring water
or take in sunset like supper,
those who don't want to change,

let them sleep.

This Love is beyond the study of theology,
that old trickery and hypocrisy.
If you want to improve your mind that way,

sleep on.
I've given up on my brain.
I've torn the cloth to shreds
and thrown it away.

If you're not completely naked,
wrap your beautiful robe of words
around you, and sleep.

Mevlana Rumi, Persian poet and mystic, 1207–1273
Translated from the Persian
by Coleman Barks and John Moyne

WINDOWS AND DOORS

for Jo

I dreamt of you standing before a window by the sea
in a place that sounded something like Brittany.
You were gazing with your thousand-yard stare
at ten-thousand-year-old bluestone megaliths,
which were poised along the shore like ancient sentinels,
strong and steady, as you make me feel
when we walk together, hands entwined,
with the growing strength of oaks
sending out life-seeking roots
through solid rock,

And then you murmured,
I knew you would be the one.

Those dreamquake words rumbled in me
as if another late-night California tremor
had shaken our house on the hill.
When my eyes opened our world
wasn't shattered, nothing was destroyed.
You were standing by the window in a wispy white dress,
sunlight blithely dancing on your bare shoulders

and spangling your long black hair.
My eyes kissed your windblown soul.
You turned to me and playfully asked
Where have you been?

As if you didn't know
about the hidden door
in our house of dreams.

PHIL COUSINEAU

Once in the frozen hours of night
While the Great Bear circled Arktouros
And mortals lay drugged with sleep,
Eros stood at my gate, knocking.
"Who is pounding on my door?" I said.
"You are splitting my dreams."
"Open up. I'm only a child.
Don't be alarmed," Eros called in.
"I'm dripping wet and lost
and the night is black and moonless."
Hearing his words I pitied him
and quickly lit a candle.
Opening a door I saw a boy
with bow, wings and quiver.
I sat him down by the fire
and warmed his hands with my own,
And squeezed water from his hair.
When he recovered from the cold
he said, "Let's test the string."
He drew and struck me square
in the groin like a gadfly.
He leapt up laughing with scorn:

"Stranger, let us be happy.
My bow is unharmed, but you
Will have trouble with your heart."

ATTRIBUTED TO ANACREON, 570–488 B.C.E.
TRANSLATED FROM ANCIENT GREEK
BY WILLIS BARNSTONE

SONNET 27

Weary with toil, I haste me to my bed,
The dear repose for limbs with travel tired;
But then begins a journey in my head
To work my mind, when body's work's expired:
For then my thoughts, from far where I abide,
Intend a zealous pilgrimage to thee,
And keep my drooping eyelids open wide,
Looking on darkness which the blind do see:
Save that my soul's imaginary sight
Presents thy shadow to my sightless view,
Which, like a jewel hung in ghastly night,
Makes black night beauteous and her old face new.
    Lo! thus, by day my limbs, by night my mind,
    For thee, and for myself, no quiet find.

WILLIAM SHAKESPEARE,
ENGLISH POET, PLAYWRIGHT, 1564–1616

In the summer of the year 1797, the Author, then in ill health, had retired to a lonely farmhouse between Porlock and Linton on the Exmoor confines of Somerset and Devonshire. In consequence of a slight indisposition, an anodyne [laudanum] had been prescribed, from the effects of which he fell asleep in his chair at the moment that he was reading the following sentence, or words of the same substance, in *Purchas's Pilgrimage*: "Here the Khan Kubla commanded a palace to be built, and a stately garden thereunto: and thus ten miles of fertile ground were enclosed with a wall." The author continued for about three hours in a profound sleep, at least of the external senses, during which time he has the most vivid confidence that he could not have composed less than from two- to three-hundred lines, if that indeed can be called composition in which all the images rose up before him as things, with a parallel production of the correspondent expressions, without any sensation or consciousness of effort. On awaking he appeared to himself to have a distinct recollection of the whole, and taking his pen, ink, and paper, instantly and eagerly wrote down the lines that are here preserved. At this moment he was unfortunately called out by a person on business from Porlock, and detained by him above an hour, and on his return to his room, found, to his no small surprise and mortification, that though he still retained some vague and dim recollection of the general purport of the vision, yet, with the exception of some eight or ten scattered lines and images, all the rest had passed away like the images on the surface of a stream into which a stone had been cast, but, alas! without the after restoration of the latter:

Then all the charm
Is broken—all that phantom world so fair
Vanishes, and a thousand circlets spread,
And each misshape[s] the other. Stay awhile,
Poor youth! Who scarcely dar'st lift up
    thine eyes—
The stream will soon renew its smoothness,
    soon
The visions will return! And lo! he stays,
And soon the fragments dim of lovely forms
Come trembling back, unite, and now once
    more
The pool becomes a mirror.

Yet from the still surviving recollections in his mind, the Author has frequently purposed to finish for himself what had been originally, as it were, given to him....

As a contrast to this vision, I have annexed a fragment [*Kubla Khan:*

A Vision in a Dream. A Fragment] of a very different character, describing with equal fidelity the dream of pain and disease.

SAMUEL TAYLOR COLERIDGE,
ENGLISH POET, CRITIC, AND PHILOSOPHER, 1772–1834

VISITING MY BROTHER
ONE SUMMER NIGHT AFTER RAIN

My brother carries his little girl
I carry his little boy
rubbing sleep from their eyes
over the wet lawn
in their pajamas
with flashlights—
looking for worms!

JEFF PONIEWAZ, AMERICAN POET

LOOKING AT THEM ASLEEP

When I come home late at night and go in to kiss the children,
I see my girl with her arm curled around her head,
her face deep in unconsciousness—so
deeply centered she is in her dark self,
her mouth slightly puffed like one sated but
slightly poured like one who hadn't had enough,
her eyes so closed you would think they have rolled the
iris around to face the back of her head,
the eyeball marble-naked under that
thick satisfied desiring lid,
she lies on her back in abandon and sealed completion,
and the son in his room, oh the son he is sideways in his bed,
one knee up as if he is climbing
sharp stairs up into the night.
and under his thin quivering eyelids you
know his eyes are wide open and
staring and glazed, the blue in them so
anxious and crystally in all this darkness, and his
mouth is open, he is breathing hard from the climb
and panting a bit, his brow is crumpled
and pale, his long fingers curved,
his hand open, and in the center of each hand
the dry dirty boyish palm

resting like a cookie. I look at him in his
quest, the thin muscles of his arms
passionate and tense, I look at her with her
face like the face of a snake who has swallowed a deer,
content, content—and I know if I wake her she'll
smile and turn her face toward me though
half asleep and open her eyes and I
know if I wake him he'll jerk and say Don't and sit
up and stare about him in blue
unrecognition, oh my Lord how I
know these two. When love comes to me and says
What do you know, I say This girl, this boy.

SHARON OLDS, AMERICAN POET

NIGHT SONG

Spring; the air is October.
The night-swathed maples linger in mid-breeze

and everyone seems to be sleeping
or away.

and my belly, the whole middle of my body
swells, as when I carried you—

or later, like your body
as it passed into night.

I was your mother,
and night passed through me, into night.

No one can touch me.
No one can touch me.

SARAH MACLAY, AMERICAN POET

After the candles were bought Kant prosecuted his studies till nearly ten o'clock. A quarter of an hour before retiring for the night, he withdrew his mind as much as possible from every class of thoughts which demanded any exertion or energy of attention, on the principle, that by stimulating him and exciting him too much, such thoughts would be apt to cause wakefulness; and the slightest interference with his customary hour of falling asleep was in the highest degree unpleasant to him. Happily this was with him a very rare occurrence. He undressed himself without his servant's assistance; but in such an order and with such a Roman regard to decorum and the Greek *to arête* [excellence] that he was always ready at a moment's warning to make his appearance without embarrassment to himself or to others. This done, he lay down on a mattress, and wrapped himself up in a quilt, which in summer was always of cotton; in autumn, of wool; at the setting in of winter, he used both; and, against severe cold, he protected himself by one of eiderdown, of which the part which covered his shoulders was not stuffed with feathers, but padded, or rather wadded closely with layers of wool. Long practice had taught him a very dexterous mode of *nesting* and enswathing himself in the bedclothes. First of all, he sat down on the bedside; then with an agile motion he vaulted obliquely into his lair; next he drew one corner of the bed-clothes under his left shoulder, and passing it below his back brought it round so as to rest under his right shoulder; fourthly, by a particular *tour d'adresse*, he treated the other corner in the same way; and finally contrived to roll it round his whole person. Thus, swathed like a mummy, or (as I used to tell him) self-involved like the silk worm in its cocoon, he awaited the approach of sleep, which generally came on immediately.

THOMAS DE QUINCEY, ENGLISH ESSAYIST, 1785–1859

A DREAM WITHIN A DREAM

Take this kiss upon the brow!
And, in parting from you now,
Thus much let me avow—
You are not wrong, who deem
That my days have been a dream;
Yet if hope has flown away
In a night, or in a day,
In a vision, or in none,
Is it therefore the less *gone*?
All that we see or seem
Is but a dream within a dream.

I stand amid the roar
Of a surf-tormented shore,
And I hold within my hand
Grains of the golden sand—
How few! Yet how they creep
Through my fingers to the deep,
While I weep—while I weep!
O, God! can I not grasp
Them with a tighter clasp?
O, God! can I not save
One from the pitiless wave?
Is *all* that we see or seem
But a dream within a dream?

EDGAR ALLAN POE, AMERICAN WRITER, 1809–1849

From breakfast on through all the day
At home among friends I stay,
But every night I go abroad
Afar into the land of Nod.

All by myself I have to go,
With none to tell me what to do—
All alone beside the streams
And up the mountain-sides of dreams.

The strangest things are there for me,
Both things to eat and things to see,
And many frightening sights abroad
Till morning in the land of Nod.

Try as I like to find the way,
I never can get back by day,
Nor can remember plain and clear
The curious music that I hear.

ROBERT LOUIS STEVENSON, SCOTTISH WRITER, 1850–1894

THE SENTINEL IN LOVE

A soldier was in love. Even if not on guard he could never rest. At last, a friend begged him to have a few hours' sleep. The soldier said; "I am a sentinel, and I am in love. How can I rest? A soldier on duty must not sleep, so it is an advantage to him to be in love. Each night love puts me to the test, and thus I can stay awake and keep watch on the fort. This love is a friend to the sentinel, for wakefulness becomes part of him; he who reaches this state will ever be on the watch."

Do not sleep, O man, if you are striving for knowledge of yourself. Guard well the fortress of your heart, for there are thieves everywhere. Do not let brigands steal the jewel you carry. True knowledge will come to him who can stay awake. He who patiently keeps watch will be aware when God comes near him. True lovers who wish to surrender themselves to the intoxication of love go apart together. He who has spiritual love holds in his hand the keys of the two worlds. If one is a woman one becomes a man; and if one is a man one becomes a deep ocean.

FARID UD-DIN ATTAR, 1110–1230
RENDERED INTO ENGLISH BY C.S. NOTT FROM THE FRENCH TRANSLATION OF
GARCIN DE TASSY

POSTCARD FROM THE NEW DELHI NIGHT

One thin candle warped by the heat of day now burns in the heat of night by a grass mat on an open flat roof top in a New Delhi neighborhood. We can't see the local night watchman but listen to his stick strike the street with reassurance. The street is warm concrete...as is the roof top which now hosts a trail of ants seemingly roused by the little candle flame in the heavy still air. It is about midnight and finally nearly cool enough to sleep till sunrise. But then, once the sun peaks over the roof lines and falls on our mat it will within minutes be too hot to sleep any more. Paid 12 cents for a simple shave yesterday, only costs a nickel in the country. But we've left the country and are preparing to fly to Bangkok, unless the evidence we're to see on Saturday confirms our friend's assertion that there are exceptional carpet buys way up about 35 miles from the Tibetan border. It must be daylight where you are, hope you enjoy today as much as we already did. A family sleeps on this roof with us; thousands sleep in the street, some by choice. In the family's courtyard below a fat dog sprawls in the dim shadows, and in the distance an occasional scooter rickshaw purrs through the dark. Downstairs they will begin to make the first of many morning cups of tea about 5 a.m., before the heat of light comes and before the servant boy Ram arises. On the other side is Krishna as perceived in certain (and uncertain) places.

JAMES BOTSFORD, AMERICAN LAWYER-POET

SONNET 43

When most I wink, then do mine eyes best see,
For all the day they view things unrespected;
But when I sleep, in dreams they look on thee,
And darkly bright are bright in dark directed.
Then thou, whose shadow shadows doth make bright,
How would thy shadow's form form happy show
To the clear day with thy much clearer light,
When to unseeing eyes thy shade shines so!
How would, I say, mine eyes be blessed made
By looking on thee in the living day,
When in dead night thy fair imperfect shade
Through heavy sleep on sightless eyes doth stay!
All days are nights to see till I see thee,
And nights bright days when dreams do show thee me.

WILLIAM SHAKESPEARE,
ENGLISH POET, PLAYWRIGHT, 1564–1616

I dream'd we both were in a bed
Of Roses, almost smothered:
The warmth and sweetness had me there
Made lovingly familiar:
But that I heard thy sweet breath say,
Faults done by night will blush by day:
I kist thee (panting) and I call
Night to the Record! That was all.
But ah! If empty dreams so please,
Love give me more such nights as these.

ROBERT HERRICK, ENGLISH POET, 1591–1674

1.
Tail lights on the highway
Going home for the holidays
Driving through this winter night
I should be there by morning light
Spend a few days in my hometown
See some old friends, make the rounds
And if I see her that's okay
Just say hello, happy holidays

Chorus:
I'm dreaming while I drive
Dreaming back to another time
We all live so many lives
I'm dreaming while I drive

2.
Pull over to a night café
Cup of coffee and I'm on my way
Snow starts falling but the roads are clear
Slow and steady, that'll get me there
Christmas days long ago
I remember the falling snow

Children sang those old melodies
The world was white and red and green

Chorus:
I'm dreaming while I drive
Dreaming back to another time
We all live so many lives
I'm dreaming while I drive

3.
These old roads have changed with time
They got wider and more white lines
I guess I've changed, at least that much
I got a little wider, a little more out of touch
But count your blessings, they always say
Just be grateful for one more day
This old life's been a winding road
There's some things I take with me when I go

Chorus:
I'm dreaming while I drive
Dreaming back to another time
We've all lived so many lives
I'm dreaming while I drive

RB MORRIS, AMERICAN WRITER, MUSICIAN, AND ACTOR

A RENAISSANCE REMEDY FOR SLEEPLESSNESS

It often happens to melancholics, especially to those who are men of letters, that their brains become dried out, and they become weak from long nights of sleeplessness. Because there is nothing that increases black bile trouble more than prolonged sleeplessness, one must take great pains to find help for this problem. These people should eat lettuce after some of their meals, together with a little bread and a little saffron. They should drink pure Wine after the lettuce, and they should not stay up working beyond that hour. When they go to bed, they should take this formula: take two parts white poppy-seed, one part lettuce seed, balsam, and saffron, a half dram of each, and six parts sugar, dissolve and cook it all in poppy-juice. Eat two drams of this stuff, and at the same time drink some poppy-juice or wine. You can also smear on your face and temples an oil of violets, and if you do not have any use camphor; the same with milk and oil of almond, and violet water. Move the nostrils with the fragrance of saffron and camphor, and with clippings from sweet fruit trees. Go very easy on vinegar, but use a lot of rosewater.

Smooth your bed with the leaves of cool plants. Delight your ears with pleasant songs and sounds. You can dampen your head a lot with a little bath in some water in which perhaps you have cooked the fruits of poppies, lettuce, purlain, mallows, roses, vines, and the leaves of reeds, adding camomile. Having sweetened your bathwater with all these things, get your whole body wet with it, including arms and legs.

Furthermore, it is especially good to drink milk mixed with sugar, on an empty stomach, of course, if the stomach will tolerate it. This dampening business works wonderfully for melancholics, even for those who get enough sleep. Remember that almond milk should be very familiar to your table.

MARSILIO FICINO,
ITALIAN AUTHOR, ARCHITECT, 1433–1499
TRANSLATED FROM THE ITALIAN BY CHARLES BOER

THE NIGHT OF THE DIAPHANOUS DREAM

My diaphanous white skirts swirled around me and flowed like liquid, undulating rhythmically as I danced ecstatically in the silky blackness of the diamond-studded night sky. I was vast, immortal, and extraordinarily joyous. I was Home.

As my eyes slowly opened I wasn't sure if I was dreaming awake again. After three months of sleeping under this magnificent sky-blanket in Big Sur, I began to merge and become one with the billions of stars, the planets and galaxies, and the exquisite moon caressing my face as I slept.

For hours I would lie quietly on my back staring into the vastness before dozing off. Each night my "dream eyes" were perceiving more of this majesty moving throughout the darkness. Both dreaming and awake, I watched as the earth turned in her steady rotation and the Universe ever changing in his. Both were reveling in their Sufi dance as they whirled passionately with one another.

On my night of the diaphanous dream I saw a stunning display of the Milky Way shimmering and swimming above me. She was just as I had seen her, just as I had danced her. I had *become* her. I was One with the vast silence of the cosmos, no longer anchored to my earthly form. I was one with our mother galaxy, the Milky Way in her stunning 120,000 light-years across. How rapturously she expends her milky gasses and dust to create this extraordinarily beautiful home for us. We are all stars embedded on the rim of her great flowing skirt. We *are* made of stardust.

My DNA was permanently recalibrated during those astoundingly beautiful months of sleeping in the Ventana Wilderness under the vast and glorious dome of our Universe. Dark matter became a soothing comfort, and the stars and moonlight, my "soul vitamins." I would walk the trail up to my tree house in the moonlight to memorize the feel of the path so I could traverse it comfortably again with no moon. The steep ravine that dropped off the trail held no fear for me, as I was One with the earth beneath my feet and was connected to the pull of the stars above which guided me—even with my eyes closed.

I long for the dark, safe womb of the Universe, the purity and freedom from form. I long for the primordial blackness from where the spark of life was ignited, and for the infinite potential of Source.

Without this infinite darkness there is no light. Without the night we could not see the stars and revel in the mystery of it all.

JOANNE WARFIELD,
AMERICAN PHOTOGRAPHER AND ARTIST

Is there a method for cultivating mindfulness? There are many methods. The one I have chosen is gratefulness, which can be practiced, cultivated, learned. And as we grow in gratefulness, we grow in mindfulness. Before I open my eyes in the morning, I remind myself that I have eyes to see while millions of my brothers and sisters are blind—most because of conditions that could be improved if our human family would come to its senses and spend its resources reasonably, equitably. If I open my eyes with this thought, chances are that I will be more grateful for the gift of sight and more alert to the needs of those who lack the gift. Before I turn off the light in the evening, I jot down one thing for which I have never before been grateful. I have done this for years, and the supply still seems inexhaustible.

Gratefulness brings joy to my life. How could I find joy in what I take for granted? So I stop "taking for granted," and there is no end to the surprises I find. A grateful attitude is a creative one, because, in the final analysis, opportunity is the gift within the gift of every moment—the opportunity to see and hear and smell and touch and taste with pleasure.

There is no closer bond than the one that gratefulness celebrates, the bond between giver and thanksgiver. Everything is a gift. Grateful living is a celebration of the universal give-and-take of life, a limitless yes to belonging.

Can our world survive without gratefulness? Whatever the answer, one thing is certain: to say an unconditional yes to the mutual belonging of all beings will make this a more joyful world. This is the reason yes is my favorite synonymous for God.

BROTHER DAVID STEINDL-RAST,
BENEDICTINE MONK AND WRITER

In my regular life—the one I call "real"—I sleep every night at 8:30 p.m. My body gets me up early in the morning, as soon as it is light, and by the time darkness falls I'm starting to lose consciousness, fast. All the corners of the night, therefore, everything associated with the sleeping world, is as foreign to me as Antarctica. In my regular life I know the time so well that I can usually tell the hour to the minute without looking at my watch.

Under jet lag, however, all that is thrown into convulsions. Not just the steady routine, the sense of clear divisions, the ability to get on with the world, in synch with it. No, something deeper is dissolved. I get off a plane, 17 hours out of joint, and tell naked secrets to a person I don't trust. A friend starts talking about her days—her plans, her friends, the things she wants to do—and tears start welling in my eyes, in a restaurant. I can't sleep at night (because I've been sleeping in the day), and so I try to go through my routine, as I might in the normal world. But I write the wrong name on the uncharacteristically emotional letter. I shower the stranger with endearments. When the lady at the bank offers me a $3000 credit for the $30,000 check I've given her (a large part of my yearly income), I smile and say, "Have a nice day."

I often think that I've traveled into a deeply foreign country under jet lag, somewhere more mysterious in its way than India or Morocco. A place that no human had ever been until 40 or so years ago, and yet, now, a place where more and more of us spend more and more of our lives. It's not quite a dream state, and yet it's certainly not wakefulness; and though it seems another continent we're visiting, there are no maps or guidebooks yet to this other world. There are not even any clocks.

I live these days in Japan, and my mother, who is in her 70s and lives alone, stays in California. Every time I want to look in on her, therefore, I get on a plane and take the 10-hour flight across the Pacific. But for a week—at least—after I arrive, I'm not myself. I look like myself, perhaps, I may sound something like myself, but I'm wearing my sweater inside-out and coming out from the unremarkable movie *Bounce* very close to tears. I'm not the person I might be when I'm antic or giddy or have been up too late; I'm a kind of spectral being floating above myself.

Every time I fly back to Japan, I become the meridian opposite of that impostor, a Sebaldian night wanderer who cannot be trusted to read or write anything for at least another week. If I visit my mother four times a year, therefore—a reasonable thing to do in the ordinary human scheme of things—I spend eight weeks a year, or almost a sixth of my life, in this nowhere state. Not quite on the ground, yet not entirely off it.

PICO IYER, BRITISH ESSAYIST, NOVELIST, AND WANDERER

SLEEPWALKING

There are some bizarre studies about sleepwalking. I think we have all heard of the lady guest in a great house who woke in the small hours to hear the breathing and moving of a male presence. On the coverlet she could feel objects being placed in order and with deliberation. She did not dare stir. Wisely she fainted. She came to at dawn to find that the butler had walked in his sleep and laid the table for fourteen on her bed. Lawrence Wright, the bed expert, tells of the baronet in Hampshire who went to bed every night in a shirt and every morning woke stark naked. There was no trace of the garment anywhere. After hundreds of shirts had disappeared in this way, he asked a friend to watch over his sleep. The friend did so and, as the clock struck one, observed the baronet got out bed, light a candle, and walk out of the room. The friend followed him a fair distance to the stable-yard, where the baronet took off his shirt and, using a pitch-fork, burned it in a dungheap. He then returned, still fast asleep, to his naked bed.

One morning I got up to find the following verses scrawled in lipstick on my dining room wall:

> *Let his carbon gnoses be up right*
> *And wak all followers to his light*

The writing was my own and lipstick my wife's. Some people talk of the inspiration of sleep and assert that there is great wisdom to be tapped in the unconscious mind. If this couplet is a specimen of this wisdom let me stay conscious. I knew a man who woke up in the night to find he had discovered in sleep the key to the universe. He scrawled on a pad kept on his bedside table the mystical unlocking words. Waking he read them: "All a matter of demisemiquavers. Make much of this."

ANTHONY BURGESS, 1917–1993

PART V

MORNING HAS BROKEN

*"Morning has broken
like the first morning....
Praise for the singing,
praise for the morning."*

— CAT STEVENS

O ne of the biggest surprises of my son's first year at Cathedral School for Boys in San Francisco was attending a service with his first grade class at Grace Cathedral and hearing them sing the Cat Stevens 1960s hit "Morning is Broken." I found it deeply moving to hear the boys singing a song that was considered a simple pop tune when I was in school, but was now enshrined as a hymn in the original sense of the word, a song of praise, to the beauty of daybreak. The soft-spun words help us cross the last threshold of our journey into the rays of the day.

That song's irrepressibly optimistic tone is captured beautifully in the strangely beautiful cadence and alliteration of a single line by the great poet Gerard Manley Hopkins, who wrote, "I wake and feel the fell of dark, not day."

In his seventeenth-century play, *La Vida Es Sueño (Life Is a Dream)*,

Pedro Calderón de la Barca anticipated much of today's magic realism and surrealistic literature. Writing as hypnotically as Jorge Borges or Isabelle Allende would two centuries later, Calderón revealed that when he slept...he saw...that he dreamt...when he was awake:

> *"We live in a world so strange,*
> *That to live is only to dream.*
> *He who lives, dreams his life*
> *Until he wakes. This much*
> *Experience has taught me."*

And now we can ask ourselves what we have brought back from our own elliptical night journey? "Is the rising light daybreak," asks the Persian poet Bibi Hayati, "or the reflection of your face?" Is Coach in the long-running television comedy *Cheers* just crazy or madly inspired when he confides to Sam the bartender, "I think I had insomnia last night, but I don't remember because I fell asleep."

For those night writers in this final stretch of the night, "the morning hour has gold in its mouth," as imagined in the German proverb. Night has been endured, outlasted, literally *incorporated*, taken into the body. The morning star flickers on the horizon. Slowly, bewilderedly, we emerge from the shadowlands. On the morning of his sacred vision, the Oglala Sioux shaman and missionary Black Elk heard the sun singing as it rose and felt it calling for a song from him. Strengthened by his lifted voice, he foresaw that by walking in a sacred manner as dawn was breaking he could say, "My day, I have made it holy." As the Winnebago shaman Reuben Snake loved to say about uplifting thoughts like that, "Aho!"

The night journey is a flight of faith. Charles Lindbergh, in his memoir *The Spirit of St Louis*, reveals the mysteries of how time stopped and distance too, who "Set my mind on the sunrise—'desire for sleep' never so badly." A carousel of belief that what goes around comes around. The Kentucky priest and poet Father Gary Young encapsulates the bold optimism of this final turn of the book in his marvelous poem, "In My Own House I Am a Stranger at Midnight," which concludes, "This midnight belongs to me—and I have the oil." And as is appropriate the final word goes to the Bard in *The Tempest*, "We are such stuff / As dreams are made on, and our little life / Is rounded with a sleep."

Comes around, turning, rounded: these are not accidental verbs. They were chosen precisely to describe the slow ratcheting of the night back into the light. They signal the exaltation that comes from completing the long night's journey into the day.

Many years ago, my father responded to a nervous letter I had sent to him about my woebegone efforts as a young writer by sending me a cartoon strip by Charles Schultz. Good ol' Charlie Brown is lying in bed with a full moon rising outside his window. The first balloon dialogue above his bald-but-for-a-single-hair head reads: "Sometimes I lie awake at night, and I ask, 'Where have I gone wrong?'" The second panel shows him frowning in permanent disappointment and the dialogue reads: "Then a voice says to me, 'This is going to take more than one night.'"

As such, these night writers round out our collection of night writing and, as Sam Cooke once crooned, "Bring it on home."

To what prayers and poetry, what cries from the heart and praise from the soul, will we listen, if not these, if not now, as dawn is breaking once more, and the flame from our lamp flutters and goes out, and encourages us to greet the new day?

What the long night's journey into day teaches us is that if you gaze long enough into the darkness, you will eventually see everything.

DAWN

Suddenly
Dawn in gold sandals

Sappho, Greek poet, 625-570 B.C.E.
Translated by Willis Barnstone

END OF A PARTY

Beautiful
He throws peace into frenzy
and exhaustion and dumbs the mind.
Sitting
But come, my friends.
Soon daybreak.

Sappho, Greek poet, 625-570 B.C.E.
Translated by Willis Barnstone

To be spoken from bed, in the early morning, before anybody has risen.

> I will rise from sleep
> With the swiftness
> Of the raven's wingbeat.
> I will rise to meet the day
> Wa-wa.
>
> My face turns
> From the darkness,
> My eyes turn to meet
> The dawn, whitening the sky.

ORPINGALIK, INUIT SHAMAN, POET
TRANSLATED FROM NETSILKI ESKIMO
BY TOM LOWENSTEIN

TO TAN CH'IU

My friend is lodging high in the Eastern Range,
Dearly loving the beauty of valleys and hills.
At green Spring he lies in the empty woods,
And is still asleep when the sun shines on high.
A pine-tree wind dusts his sleeves and coat;
A pebbly stream cleans his heart and ears.
I envy you, who far from strife and talk
Are high-propped on a pillow of blue cloud.

LI PO, CHINESE POET, 701–762
TRANSLATED FROM THE CHINESE BY ARTHUR WALEY

FOR FLEAS, ALSO

Slowly, slowly, climb
Up and up Mount Fuji,
O snail.

Far-off mountain peaks
Reflected in its eyes:
The dragonfly.

For fleas, also, the night
Must be so very long,
So very lonely.

Stop! Don't swat the fly
Who wrings his hands,
Who wrings his feet.

With bland serenity
Gazing at the far hills:
A tiny frog.

Emerging from the nose
Of Great Buddha's statue:
A swallow.

Spring rain:
The uneaten ducks
Quack.

Red sky in the morning:
Does it gladden you,
O snail?

KOBAYASHI ISSA, JAPANESE POET, 1763–1828
TRANSLATED FROM THE JAPANESE
BY GEOFFREY BOWNAS AND ANTHONY THWAITE

THE NIGHT AT ZENSHO-JI TEMPLE

I spent the night at a temple called Zensho-ji on the outskirts of the town of Daishoji. I was still in the province of Kaga. Sora had stayed at the temple the night before and had left a poem:

> *All through the night*
> *I listened to the autumn wind*
> *In the lonely hills.*

We were only one night apart, but it seemed like a thousand miles. I, too, listened to the autumn wind as I lay awake. As dawn approached, I could hear the priests chanting. Then a gong sounded and we all went in to the refectory. Since I wanted to reach Echizen Province that same day, I started to leave in a great hurry, but a young monk came running down the steps after me with some paper and an ink stone. Just then, some leaves from a willow tree in the garden fluttered to the ground.

> *Your kindness to repay,*
> *Would I might sweep the fallen*
> *Willow leaves away.*

My straw sandals were already tied on, so I did not even take the time to read over my hurried lines.

BASHO, 1644–1694
TRANSLATED FROM THE JAPANESE BY DOROTHY BRITTON

THE THROAT OF DAWN

What if I'm the son of a 92-year-old man
who can hardly walk from the kitchen to
the couch in the home where I grew up,
which is flooded by a storm whose wet arms
covered a thousand miles. What if I can't
reach him because the phone he can't find
is wet and has no power. What if a month
later I travel to Cambodia on a trip that took
five years to save for, and out of breath I stare
for an hour at a thousand-year-old face carved
at Angkor Wat. What if that eyeless face makes
me question what I've done with my life. What
if I can't stop thinking of my father struggling
to pick up a spoon. What if on the plane home
the woman next to me dreams of her mother's
mother picking lemons in Sicily. What if the
thousand angels, who never rest, work in each
of us, the way immune cells rush to the site of
a wound. What if all this keeps me from sleep-
ing. What if I fear that I will never sleep again.
What if, as the plane slips through the throat
of dawn, it comes to me that we're not sup-
posed to find something new all the time,

but weave each truth we find into a strong,
beautiful rope that the next generation can
climb. What if I admit that I found nothing
to bring home to my father, except the heart
of a son carved out by time. What if everything
we do and everywhere we go is for this end.
What if the heart carved out is what
can shelter us from the storm.

MARK NEPO, AMERICAN POET AND PHILOSOPHER

MY IMMORTAL BELOVED

Good morning, on July 7 [1801]

Though still in bed my thoughts go out to you, my Immortal
Beloved, now and then joyfully, then sadly, waiting to learn whether
or not fate will hear us. I can live only wholly with you or not at
all—yes, I am resolved to wander so long away from you until I
can fly to your arms and say that I am really at home with you,
and can send my soul, enwrapped in you, into the land of spirits.
—Yes, unhappily it must be so—you will be the more resolved since
you know my fidelity—to you, no one can ever again possess my

heart—none—never—Oh, God! why is it necessary to part from one whom one so loves and yet my life in W. [Vienna] is now a wretched life—your love makes me at once the happiest and the unhappiest of men—at my age, I need a steady, quiet life—can that be so under our conditions? My angel, I have just been told that the mail coach goes every day—and I must close at once so that you may receive the letter at once. Be calm, only by a calm consideration of our existence can we achieve our purpose to live together— be calm—love me—today—yesterday—what tearful longings for you—you—you—my life—my all—farewell—Oh continue to love me—never misjudge the most faithful heart of your beloved.

ever thine
ever thine
ever for each other

LUDWIG VAN BEETHOVEN,
GERMAN COMPOSER, 1770–1827
UNSENT LETTER TO UNIDENTIFIED INAMORATA

"Curiouser and curiouser!" cried Alice (she was so much surprised, that for the moment she quite forgot how to speak good English). "Now I'm opening out like the largest telescope that ever was! Good-bye, feet!" (for when she looked down at her feet, they seemed to be almost out of sight, they were getting so far off).

"Oh, my poor little feet, I wonder who will put on your shoes and stockings for you now, dears? I'm sure *I* shan't be able! I shall be a great deal too far off to trouble myself about you: you must manage the best way you can; —but I must be kind to them," thought Alice, "or perhaps they won't walk the way I want to go! Let me see: I'll give them a new pair of boots every Christmas."

And she went on planning to herself how she would manage it. "They must go by the carrier," she thought; "and how funny it'll seem, sending presents to one's own feet! And how odd the directions will look!

> ALICE'S RIGHT FOOT, ESQ.
> HEARTHRUG,
> NEAR THE FENDER,
> (WITH ALICE'S LOVE).

Oh dear, what nonsense I'm talking!"

Just then her head struck against the roof of the hall: in fact she was now more than nine feet high, and she at once took up the little golden key and hurried off to the garden door.

Poor Alice! It was as much as she could do, lying down on one side, to look through into the garden with one eye; but to get through was more hopeless than ever: she sat down and began to cry again.

"You ought to be ashamed of yourself," said Alice, "a great girl like you," (she might well say this), "to cry in this way! Stop this instant, I tell you!" But she went on all the same, shedding gallons of tears, until there was a large pool all round her, about four inches deep and reaching half down the hall.

After a time she heard a little pattering of feet in the distance, and she hastily dried her eyes to see what was coming. It was the White Rabbit returning, splendidly dressed, with a pair of white kid gloves in one hand and a large fan in the other: he came trotting along in a great hurry, muttering to himself as he came, "Oh! the Duchess, the Duchess! Oh! won't she be savage if I've kept her waiting!" Alice felt so desperate that she was ready to ask help of any one; so, when the Rabbit came near her, she began, in a low, timid voice, "If you please, sir—" The Rabbit started violently, dropped the white kid gloves and the fan, and skurried away into the darkness as hard as he could go.

Alice took up the fan and gloves, and, as the hall was very hot, she kept fanning herself all the time she went on talking: "Dear, dear! How queer everything is to-day! And yesterday things went on just as usual. I wonder if I've been changed in the night? Let me think: was I the same when I got up this morning? I almost think I can remember feeling a little different. But if I'm not the same, the next question is, Who in the world am I? Ah, *THAT'S* the great puzzle!" And she began thinking over all the children she knew that were of the same age as herself, to see if she could have been changed for any of them.

"I'm sure I'm not Ada," she said, "for her hair goes in such long ringlets, and mine doesn't go in ringlets at all; and I'm sure I can't be Mabel, for I know all sorts of things, and she, oh! she knows such a very little! Besides, *SHE'S* she, and I'm I, and—oh dear, how puzzling it all is! I'll try if I know all the things I used to know. Let me see: four times five is twelve, and four times six is thirteen, and four times seven is—oh dear! I shall never get to twenty at that rate! However, the Multiplication Table doesn't signify: let's try Geography. London is the capital of Paris, and Paris is the capital of Rome, and Rome—no, *THAT'S* all wrong, I'm certain! I must have been changed for Mabel! I'll try and say 'How doth the little—' and she crossed her hands on her lap as if she were saying lessons, and began to repeat it, but her voice sounded hoarse and strange, and the words did not come the same as they used to do:

'How doth the little crocodile
Improve his shining tail,
And pour the waters of the Nile
On every golden scale!
How cheerfully he seems to grin,
How neatly spread his claws,

And welcome little fishes in
With gently smiling jaws!'"

LEWIS CARROLL,
ENGLISH WRITER AND MATHEMATICIAN, 1832–1898

IT GAVE ME THE DARING

(On Lalla's own songs)

I didn't trust it for a moment,
but I drank it anyway,
the wine of my own poetry.

It gave me the daring to take hold
of the darkness and tear it down
and cut it into little pieces.

LALLA, KASHMIRI MYSTIC POET, 1320–1392
TRANSLATED FROM THE KASHMIRI BY COLEMAN BARKS

WAKE!

I

Wake! For the Sun who scatter'd into flight
The Stars before him from the Field of Night,
Drives Night along with them from Heaven and strikes
The Sultan's Turret with a Shaft of Light.

IX

Each Morn a thousand Roses brings, you say;
Yes, but where leaves the Rose of Yesterday?
And this first Summer month that brings the Rose
Shall take Jamshyd and Kaikobad away.

XVII

Think, in this batter'd Caravanserai
Whose Portals are alternate Night and Day,
How Sultan after Sultan with his Pomp
Abode his destined Hour, and went his way.

LXVIII

We are no other than a moving row
Of Magic Shadow-shapes that come and go
Round with the Sun-illumined Lantern held
In Midnight by the Master of the Show;

LXIX

But helpless Pieces of the Game He plays
Upon this Chequer-board of Nights and Days;
Hither and thither moves, and checks, and slays,
And one by one back in the Closet lays.

LXX

The Ball no question makes of Ayes and Noes,
But Here or There as strikes the Player goes;
And He that toss'd you down into the Field,
He knows about it all—He knows—HE knows!

LXXI

The Moving Finger writes; and, having writ,
Moves on: nor all your Piety nor Wit
Shall lure it back to cancel half a Line,
Nor all your Tears wash out a Word of it.

Omar Khayyam,
Persian philosopher, astronomer, poet, 1048–1131
Translated from the Persian by Edward Fitzgerald

And a poet said, Speak to us of Beauty,
    and he answered:
Where shall you seek beauty, and how shall
you find her unless she herself be your way
and your guide?

And how shall you speak of her except she
be the weaver of your speech?

The aggrieved and the injured say, "Beauty
is kind and gentle.

Like a young mother half-shy of her own
glory, she walks among us."

And the passionate say, "Nay, beauty is a
thing of might and dread.

Like the tempest she shakes the earth beneath us
and the sky above us."

The tired and the weary say, "Beauty is of
soft whisperings. She speaks in our spirit.

Her voice yields to our silences like a faint
light that quivers in fear of the shadow."

But the restless say, "We have heard her
shouting among the mountains,

And with her cries came the sound of hoofs,
and the beating of wings and the roaring of

lions."

At night the watchmen of the city say, "Beauty shall rise with the dawn from the east."

KAHLIL GIBRAN,
LEBANESE POET, PHILOSOPHER, 1883–1931

TO AWAKEN EACH MORNING

To awaken each morning with a smile brightening my face; to greet the day with reverence for the opportunities it contains; to approach my work with a clean mind; to hold ever before me, even in the doing of little things, the Ultimate Purpose toward which I am working; to meet men and women with laughter on my lips and love in my heart; to be gentle, kind, and courteous through all the hours; to approach the night with weariness that ever woos sleep and the joy that comes from work well done—this is how I desire to waste wisely my days.

THOMAS DEKKER, ENGLISH WRITER, 1572–1632

LYING SINGLE IN BED

Rode easily to Welling, where we supped well, and had two beds in the room and so lay single, and still remember it of all nights that ever I slept in my life I never did pass a night with more epicurism of sleep; there being now and then a noise of people stirring that waked me, and then it was a very rainy night, and then I was a little weary, that what between waking and sleeping again, one after another, I never had so much content in all my life, and so my wife says it was with her.

SAMUEL PEPYS,
ENGLISH DIARIST AND MEMBER OF PARLIAMENT, 1633–1703

EACH SOUL MUST MEET THE MORNING SUN

In the life of the Indian there was only one inevitable duty—the duty of prayer—the daily recognition of the Unseen and Eternal. His daily devotions were more necessary to him than daily food. He wakes at daybreak, puts on his moccasins and steps down to the water's edge. Here he throws handfuls of clear, cold water into his face, or plunges in bodily. After the bath, he stands erect before the advancing dawn, facing the sun as it dances upon the horizon, and offers his unspoken orison. His mate may precede or follow him in his devotions, but never accompanies him. Each soul must meet the morning sun, the new sweet earth and Great Silence alone!

Whenever, in the course of the daily hunt the red hunter comes upon a scene that is strikingly beautiful or sublime—a black thundercloud with the rainbow's glowing arch above the mountain, a white waterfall in the heart of a green gorge; a vast prairie tinged with the blood-red of sunset— he pauses for an instant in the attitude of worship. He sees no need for setting apart one day in seven as a holy day, since to him all days are God's.

OHIYESA (CHARLES ALEXANDER EASTMAN), SANTEE SIOUX PHYSICIAN,
WRITER, REFORMER, 1858–1939

WAKING IN THE MONASTERY

One day when the brethren were engaged in the manual labor of the monastery. A young zealot came to the Abbot Hilarion and told him that he had become inspired with the idea of competing in saintliness with the desert fathers of times past.

The abbot sighed and looked up from his basket-weaving.

"I have a better idea."

He smiled.

"Compete with the saint you were when you woke this morning: that would be more beneficial, and," he added, "you would have a better chance of success."

GARY YOUNG, AMERICAN POET-PRIEST

ZERO IN THE DARK

The temperature was zero one recent morning, and when I went out to feed the horses just before dawn, the moon was frozen against the sky. The rim of light against the dark hills in the east looked exactly like the rim of light that forms at dusk against the dark hills in the west. The snow is dry, and there are deer tracks all across the farm, pointed hoof prints hidden deep in the snow.

Daylight is longer by only a few minutes than it was at the solstice, two weeks ago. But I keep adding to the sum in my mind. I expect the day to be longer, and so it seems. A bright day follows a dense, cloudy day, and it feels as though we have leaped ahead a month in time—until the next day, when the clouds hover only hemlock-high and snow sifts out of them almost invisibly. That's how the week goes: Forward into February! Back to December!

On bitter, clear nights, the stars look like minute ice crystals lighted by some source that requires no heat. Even when the moon is down, it is never really dark. The snow catches every particle of light there is, and a dull phosphorescence seems to spread across the pasture and into the woods. The horses stand side by side in a small cloud of their own breath, solid, opaque beasts.

It is too cold to stay outside for long in the dark. Ceilidh, the Border terrier, makes the rounds with me. The light in the chicken house has just gone off. All the gates are latched. Ceilidh tows me back toward the lights of the house, leaping the crests of plowed snow.

When we go out, we carry some warmth into the night, and when we come in, we carry some cold into the house, a vanishingly small exchange of energy in a universe of such extremes.

VERLYN KLINKENBORG, AMERICAN WRITER

THE NIGHT VIEW OF THE WORLD

"Upon the view of the world:
a day view must follow."

This is an ancient insight grounded in the experience of the race in its long journey through all the years of man's becoming. Here is no cold idea born out of the vigil of some solitary thinker in lonely retreat from the traffic of the common ways. It is not the wisdom of the book put down in ordered words by the learned and the schooled. It is insight woven into the pattern of all living things, reaching its grand apotheosis in the reflection of man gazing deep into the heart of his own experience.

That the day view follows the night view is written large in nature. Indeed it is one with nature itself. The clouds gather heavy with unshed tears; at last they burst, sending over the total landscape waters gathered from the silent offering of sea and river. The next day dawns and the whole heavens are aflame with the glorious brilliance of the sun. This is the way the rhythm moves. The fall of the year comes, then winter with its trees stripped of leaf and bud; cold winds ruthless in bitterness and sting. One day there is sleet and ice; in the silence of the night time the snow falls soundlessly—all this until at last the cold seems endless and all there is seems to be shadowy and foreboding. The earth is weary and heavy. Then something stirs—a strange new vitality pulses through everything. One can feel the pressure of some vast energy pushing, always pushing through dead branches, slumbering roots—life surges everywhere within and without. Spring has come. The day usurps the night view.

Is there any wonder that deeper than idea and concept is the insistent conviction that the night can never stay, that winter is ever moving toward the spring? Thus, when a man sees the lights go out one by one, when he sees the end of his days marked by death—his death—he *senses*, rather than knows, that even the night into which he is entering will be followed by day. It remains for religion to give this ancient wisdom phrase and symbol.

HOWARD THURMAN,
AMERICAN WRITER, THEOLOGIAN,
CIVIL RIGHTS LEADER, 1899–1981

I HAVE BEEN TRICKED

I have been tricked by flying too close
to what I thought I loved.

Now the candleflame is out, the wine spilled,
and the lovers have withdrawn
somewhere beyond my squinting.

The amount I thought I'd won, I've lost.
My prayers become bitter and all about blindness.

How wonderful it was to be for a while
with those who surrender.

Others only turn their faces one way,
then another, like a pigeon in flight.

I have known pigeons who fly nowhere,
and birds that eat grainlessness,

and a tailor who sews beautiful clothes
by tearing them to pieces.

MEVLANA RUMI, PERSIAN POET AND MYSTIC, 1207–1273
TRANSLATED FROM THE PERSIAN BY COLEMAN BARKS

DELTA DAWN
ON THE MEKONG RIVER, VIET NAM

The hazy morning sun washes everything in silhouette—
the craggy treeline across brown waters,
the early net draggers, the old woman chanting
"*banh, nuoc, com,*"—bread, water, rice—from her sampan,
school children on wobbly bicycles crossing the bank,
fruit sprouting like warts off their tree trunks.
All blend into one brown green gray shadow
pierced by lines and patches of white
where the awakening sun breaks through.
We are one in the Delta dark,
still one in this early dawn,
shouting *xin chao* and beaming smiles through the murk
until the fireball rises, burns off the clouds,
and melts us into ourselves again.

Edward Tick, American psychotherapist and poet

To the pilot of a plane without flares or landing lights, night has a meaning that no earthbound mortal can fully understand. Once he has left lighted airways there are no wayside shelters open to a flyer of the night. He can't park his plane on a cloudbank to weather out a storm, or heave over a sea anchor like the sailor and drag along slowly downwind. He's unable to control his speed like the driver of a motorcar in fog. He has to keep his craft hurtling through air no matter how black the sky or blinding storm. To land without sight is to crash.

In a period of physical awareness between these long excursions, I find the clouds around me covered with a whiter light. In the area of sky where my plane is flying, night is giving way to day. The night— so long—so short—is ending. This is the dawn of Europe, of Paris, of Le Bourget. But how dull appreciation is! Dawn—It's tremendously important. I've waited for it the whole night through. But my senses perceive it only vaguely, separately, indifferently, like pain through too weak an anaesthetic. It is intellectual knowledge, while my normal thoughts and actions are mechanical. In flesh, I'm like an automaton geared to a previously set routine.

The minute hand has just passed 1:00 a.m. It's dawn, one hour after midnight. But it's one hour after midnight only on the clock, and back at the longitude of New York where I set it before take-off in the morning—yesterday morning, it is now. The clock simply shows the number of hours I've been in the air. It relates only to my cockpit and my plane, not to time outside. It no longer marks the vital incidents of day—dawn, and noon, and sunset. My flight is disconnected from all worldly measures. It passes through different frames of time and space.

With this faint trace of day, the uncontrollable desire to sleep falls over in quilted layers. I've been staving it off with difficulty during the hours of moonlight. Now it looms all but insurmountable. This is the hour I've been dreading; the hour against which I've tried to steel myself. I know it's the beginning of my greatest test. This will be the worst time of all, this early hour of the second morning—the third morning, it is, since I've slept.

I've lost command of my eyelids. When they start to close, I can't restrain them. They shut, and I shake myself, and lift them with my fingers. I stare at the instruments, wrinkle forehead muscles tense. Lids close again regardless, stick tight as though with glue. My body has revolted from the rule of its mind. Like salt in wounds, the light of day brings back my pains. Every cell of my being is on strike, sulking in protest, claiming that nothing, nothing in the world, could be worth such effort; that man's tissue was never made for such abuse. My back is stiff; my shoulders ache, my face burns; my eyes smart. It seems impossible to go on longer. All I want in life is to throw myself down flat, stretch out—and sleep.

I've struggled with the dawn often enough before but never with such a background of fatigue. I've got to muster all my reserves, all the tricks I've learned, all remaining strength of mind for the conflict. If I can hold in air and close to course for one more hour, the sun will be over the horizon and the battle won. Each ray of light is an ally. With each moment after sunrise, vitality will increase...

I'll set my mind on the sunrise—think about that—watch the clouds brighten—the hands of the clock—count the minutes till it comes. It will be better when the full light of day has broken. It's always better after the sun comes up. As that dazzling ball of fire climbs into the sky, night's unpaid claims will pass. The desire for sleep will give way to waking habits of the day—That's always happened before—And yet, I'm not sure—It's never been like this before—I never wanted so badly—to sleep—

CHARLES LINDBERGH,
AMERICAN AVIATOR AND WRITER, 1902–1974

"[B]e cheerful, Sir.
Our revels are now ended. These our actors,
As I foretold you, were all spirits and
Are melted into air, into thin air;
And, like the baseless fabric of this vision,
The cloud-capp'd towers, the gorgeous palaces,
The solemn temples, the great globe itself,
Yea, all which it inherit, shall dissolve,
And, like this insubstantial pageant faded,
Leave not a rack behind. We are such stuff
As dreams are made on, and our little life
Is rounded with a sleep."

WILLIAM SHAKESPEARE,
ENGLISH POET, PLAYWRIGHT, 1564–1616

A day, a human day, has a certain shape and structure to it; a day, in most respects, resembles a room in which our things are ordered according to our preference. It may be empty or it may be full, but in either case it is familiar. Over here is the place where you rest (10 p.m. to 6 a.m., perhaps), over there the place where you eat or work or feel most alive. You know your way around the place so well, you can find the bathroom in the dark.

But under jet lag, of course, you lose all sense of where or who you are. You get up and walk towards the bathroom, and step into a chair. You reach towards the figure in the other bed, and then remember that she's 7000 miles away, at work. You get up for lunch, and then remember that you've eaten lunch six times already. You feel almost like an exile, a fugitive of sorts, as you walk along the hotel corridor at 4:00 a.m., while all good people are asleep, and then begin to yawn as everyone around you goes to work.

I sleep several times a day under jet lag, but it is not a normal kind of sleep. Dreams come to me that seem to belong to someone else: someone is drawing the keen edge of a sword across a throat, and there are floodlit rallies being held on the carless streets of Havana at 3:00 a.m. A Buddhist scholar I have never met in life is talking about destruction, I'm slipping into a back-room at a wedding with a long-ago girlfriend (children watching us through the window), there's talk of a house burning down. I realize at some point that all the dreams, violent and haunted, are about the dissolution of the self.

Of course, my settled and more sensible self will say, this is just the effect of irregular sleep: you're being hustled into a different state before you've even turned off the TV, in the middle of a sentence in the book. The body wasn't meant for this. It can't process images the way it does in its normal life, but is being hurried, unprepared, into the next room, everything flying out of its purse.

And yet I can't hear this self in the place I now inhabit. My stuff has been stolen—then stolen again—and I am suddenly bereft. A woman is speaking perfect Wodehouse English to me—for some reason we are on the streets of China—and I know, somehow, she speaks like that because she grew up in Fiji. A parade of ladies of the night walks past, and the woman, in a Chinese café, asks me what I should do about my stolen things...

Not long ago, in Damascus, I lived for a few days on muezzin time: long silent mornings in the Old City before dawn, walking through labyrinths of dead-end alleyways, in and out around the great mosque, and then long hot days in my room sleeping as if I were in my bed in California. Then up again in the dark, the only decoration in my room a little red arrow on the wall to show which direction Mecca was.

I went on like this for a while—watching the light come up in the mosque, seeing the city resolve itself into its shapes in the first hours of light, and then disappearing myself, down into a well—and then, after a few days, something snapped: at night, by day, I could not sleep. I stayed up all the way through a night, and the next day couldn't sleep. I drew the curtains, got into pajamas, buried myself inside the sheets. But my mind was alive now, or at least moving as with a phantom limb. Soon it was dark again, my time to wake up, and at last, at 2:00 a.m. or so, reconciled to my sleeplessness, I picked up an old copy of *Fear and Loathing in Las Vegas* and began to read.

From outside, in the fourth-floor corridor, the sound of a door being opened, then closing. Furtive rustles, a circle of whispers. The thump of a party, forbidden booze, female laughter. The ping of the elevator as it came and opened its doors; the sound of the doors closing again, the machine going up again and down. Sometimes I went to the window and, drawing the curtains, saw minarets, lit in green, the only tall monuments visible across the sleeping city. Once, putting away the story of Dr. Thompson and his Samoan, I opened the door to check the corridor, but there was no one there. No footsteps, no figures, no anything.

Hours later, I was in an Internet café in Covent Garden in London, not sure of who or where I was, having not slept for what seemed like weeks. And hours after that, in Manhattan, where I'd lived in a former life. My bags had not arrived, and so I was wearing clothes not my own, bought with an airline voucher. Outside, a drill screamed in the harsh summer light—"reconstruction," the front desk said—and I tried to push myself down into sleep, somewhere else.

A little after midnight—I was just coming to life and light now—I went out and walked to Times Square, where there was still excitement. A man was cradling his girl's head in his arm, and kissing her, kissing her softly. She stooped down to get into a cab, and he leaned in after her, kissing her again, as if to pull her back.

The cabdriver, with a conspicuous slam, put on his meter, and the car pulled away. A woman nearby was shaking her breasts at a male companion, who looked as if he belonged to another world from hers. He watched her in delight, the screens and lights all around exploding.

The man who had been kissing, kissing his girl, eyes closed, straightened himself up as the car disappeared around a corner, looked around—taxis, crowds, from every direction—and then walked across to a telephone as if to start the night anew. Crowds streamed out of theaters so you could imagine for a moment that this was New Year's Eve, the center of the world. The hushed, deserted mosque of the Old City of Damascus—I'd been there yesterday morning—was a universe away.

I walked and walked through the city in the dark, seeing a place I could easily imagine I'd never seen before, let alone lived in for four years. On 62nd and Broadway, a man, tall and dark, suddenly raced out into the street, and I stiffened, my New York instinct telling me this was an "incident." But it was just a group of cheerful men from the islands, playing cricket under the scaffolding of a prospective skyscraper at 2:00 a.m.; the man fielded the ball in the middle of the empty road and threw it back as if from a boundary in Port of Spain. Around the all-night grocery stores, the news-stands, people were speaking Hindi, Urdu, who knows what language, and epicene boys were wiggling their hips to catch the attention of taxis.

Elsewhere—last night in Damascus again—people were huddled on stoops, against buildings, bodies laid out as if no longer living, scattered across the steps of shuttered churches. A woman crouched on the steps of an all-night market, three suitcases in front of her. A man reciting to himself, outside a darkened theater. Another, wheeling a suitcase across a deserted intersection—2:57, says the digital clock outside the bank.

I'd never seen these signs of poverty, this dispossession, in all the years I'd lived here, but in the dead of night a kind of democracy comes forth. The doorman says hello to me as I pass, and the night manager of a McDonald's laughs at a drunken joke as if he's never heard it before at 3:15 a.m. On the floor of the same McDonald's, a group of kids sits in a tribal circle.

On Sixth Avenue, as I walk, a clutch of Japanese tourists, twenty or thirty, following a woman under a flag—stand silently, waiting for the light to change. As soon as it does, they walk across, en masse, as unfathomable as everything else here, off on some kind of night tour.

An all-night guard is saying something about a colleague who got lost. A tall, tall girl with a model's pony tail is hailing a cab on Eighth Avenue. A woman with a shock of blond hair, a leopardskin coat, is traipsing after a man in a suit, while another sits up and goes through her worldly possessions: a bundle of blankets beside her on the street.

I suppose I could be in Manila again, on the night side of the world.

Certainly I feel as if I've never seen this place around me, even when I lived here and worked many a night till 4 a.m. and took a cab back through the deserted streets before awakening and coming back to the office after dawn. When the light is finally up, and I go to breakfast at a fashionable hotel across from where I'm sleeping, the friend who greets me tells me that there was an incident last night, a mass murder in an all-night fast-food store in New York. Five bodies discovered in a pool of blood; it was on all the morning news shows.

"That's strange," I say (in Damascus now, Covent Garden?), "I never would have guessed it. I was out in the street last night, walking and walking; the city never looked to me so benign."

PICO IYER, BRITISH ESSAYIST, NOVELIST, AND WANDERER

For a few days of adolescent
spring I am so shy I
    want—walking down Broadway—
    to hide behind myself.
My eyes will break like an egg—
make a mess—if a woman looks at me
    and I must glance
    back. Like a small
grape I gulp these feelings
and late at night ponder the
    ceiling. Do I have
    a soul? Is that
a dream made up on the
toilet when there's nothing to read?
    My head is like
    magnifying glass. Words
are big in it, and flash
through it like a loud movie.
    I lie back, trying
    to spot myself or
any face overhead. Outside a motorcycle
roars. I look inside, plunge down.
    Only light! Then lie

for hours in dark.
Out of nervousness I pick away
The crown from my watch. I
    Saw—and lost—light.
    The soul is a
Thundering word with its profound O
And infinite I. I start to
    let go in whitening
    sleep. It is dawn.

WILLIS BARNSTONE, AMERICAN POET AND TRANSLATOR

THE BLIND WATCHMAKER

for my Grandfather Horace, son of Charlemagne

Every night the blind watchmaker rewinds the day
He is repairing the broken mechanisms of silence
He is seizing the night. With cool blue light
in his flashpoint fingertips
he is feeling for the myriad ways
that time stops, fixing the rusted springs of
old timepieces, polishing infinitesimal
jewels, nudging darkness ahead into light
He is bending low over the grand complications,
gazing through the lens of his heart
at the gauzy movements that reveal
the infinite ways time is lost
He is murmuring, asking something
of the dark source in the night
the way flashlight beams do of
the strong force beyond
distant cloud nebulae
This is how he finds time,
by *snapping* open the hidden catch

When the watchmaker appears in my nightscapes

he guides my cramped hands along the
seized gears between dusk and dawn. He is teaching
me to feel in the creases of my work-calloused fingertips
the first moment of movement in the long-stilled
second hands of watches and clocks scattered
across his desk. Every night
the steady ratcheting forward
of things, the inexorable winding
down felt in the blueness of my bones,

in no time at all

like the timeless ways
you move me
in the held-breath
seconds
before
dawn

PHIL COUSINEAU

ACKNOWLEDGEMENTS

I am indebted to Brenda Knight, a fellow nighthawk, who believed in
this book since the night at Tosca's in North Beach, San Francisco,
where we first discussed it, over, of course, one of their legendary "late
night brandies." Thanks also to RB Morris, Gregg Chadwick, Jeff
"The Dude" Dowd, Erin Byrne, Joyce Jenkins, and James Botsford,
all of whom were kind enough to discuss or read different versions
of the manuscript, or share their insights about the shadow-fretted
world after dark. I thank each of them as well for their own contribu-
tions of luminous night writing for this book. To the translator and
poet Coleman Barks, my gratitude is deep for the whirling dervish
acts of generosity by offering several newly minted translations of
Rumi, published here for the first time. Willis Barnstone has likewise
been bountiful in contributions of several translations of Greek poets
and Jorge Borges, plus one of his own recently published poems. The

incandescent pen of Pico Iyer lights up the murky corners of this book with three wonderful stories. And thanks to Alberto Manguel, who contributed two excerpts from his crepuscular *The Library at Night*, the book that has proven to be the single greatest influence on this work.

I am also grateful to the late Jane Winslow Eliot, and her husband, Alexander Eliot, to whom this book is dedicated. I have long cherished our late-night walks and talks along Venice Beach. And special thanks to Mary Anne Kuras, who has believed in me from afar.

Many thanks to all those at Viva Editions for your dedication and craft, including Kara Wuest, Kat Sanborn, and Cat Snell; my night-eyed copy editor, Kitty Florey; my publisher, Felice Newman for faith in the still of the night; Frederique Delacoste for her guidance in overall design; Scott Idleman, for his haunting blue moon cover design; and my sage agent, Amy Rennert, without whom there would be no book deal.

I would be remiss if I didn't acknowledge my local late-night café, where I completed this book, the ever-invigorating Café 901 Columbus, in North Beach, which is, like *Cheers*, "a place where everybody knows your name." And so a hearty cheers to "T" Hararah and his family of friendly baristas. While I was traveling over the last year, two other cafés helped me see the light in the dark: Bewley's on Grafton Street in Dublin, and Café Reggio, in Greenwich Village.

Finally, this book would not exist without the support of my family, Jo and Jack Cousineau, who have learned to live with the lights burning all night.

● ◐ ◑ ○ ◑ ◐ ●

Part I: The Twilight Zone

Sappho. "But I Sleep Alone" and "Evening Star," from *Bittersweet Love: Poems of Sappho*, translated by Willis Barnstone. Boston: Shambhala Press, 2006.

Tagore, Rabindranath. "Fireflies," from *Fireflies*. Hubbardston, Mass.: Asphodel Press, 2007.

Frost, Robert. "Acquainted with the Night," from *The Poetry of Robert Frost: The Collected Poems*. New York and London: Penguin Books, 1979.

Dickinson, Emily. "We Grow Accustomed to the Dark," from *Collected Poems of Emily Dickinson*, Mabel Loomis Todd and T. W. Higginson, eds. New York: Gramercy Press, 1988.

Oliver, Mary. "Last Night the Rain Spoke to Me," from *What We Know*. Boston: Da Capo Press, 2003. Reprinted by permission of Da Capo Press, a member of the Perseus Books Group. ©2002.

Hardy, Thomas. "Afterwards," from *The Collected Poems of Thomas Hardy*. Hertfordshire, England: Wordsworth Editions Ltd., 1998.

Borges, Jorge Luis. "Baruch Spinoza," from *Selected Poems*. Alexander Coleman, ed. Translated by Willis Barnstone. New York: Viking, 1999. Used by permission.

Dillard, Annie. "Each Breath of Night," from *Teaching a Stone to Talk*. New York: Harper Colophon, 1983. ©1982 by Annie Dillard.

Hopkins, Gerard Manley. "The Times Are Nightfall," from *Selected Poems*. London: Dover Publications, 2011.

Owl Woman (Juana Maxwell). "Songs of Owl Woman," from *Papago Music*. translated by Frances Densmore. Bulletin 90, Bureau of American Ethnology. Smithsonian Institution, 1929. ©1929 by Frances Densmore.

Cousineau, Phil. "Blue Mosque Reverie," from *The Book of Roads,* Sisyphus Press: 2000. Used by permission of Sisyphus Press and the author.

Rumi, Mevlana. "Night and Sleep," translated by Coleman Barks and Robert Bly. Used by permission of Coleman Barks.

Novalis. "A Hymn to the Night," translated by Dick Higgins. Kingston, N.Y.: McPherson Press, 1988.

Curtis, P.J. "The Last Prince of Thormond," from *The Music of Ghosts*. Kilnaboy, County Clare, Ireland: Old Forge Books, 2003. Used by permission of the author.

Tick, Edward. "Last Night on Santorini," from the forthcoming *Love and the Sea: Poems from the Greek World 1979–2013*. Used by permission of the author.

Blake, William. "The Tyger," from *The Collected Poems of William Blake*. W.B. Yeats, ed. Oxford: Routledge Publishing, 2002.

Bukowski, Charles. "Warm Light," from *The Last Night of the Earth Poems*. Copyright © 1992 by Charles Bukowski. Reprinted by permission of Harper-Collins Publishers.

Antler. "Mother Nursing Milky Way," from *Touch Each Other* (chapbook). Kanona, N.Y.: Foothills Publishing, 2013. Reprinted by kind permission of the author.

Agee, James. "Among the Sounds of the Night," from *A Death in the Family*, by James Agee, copyright © 1957 by The James Agee Trust. Copyright renewed

© by Mia Agee. Used by permission of Grosset & Dunlap, Inc., a division of Penguin Group (USA) LLC.

Smith, Huston. "Sunset on the Serengeti," from *And Live Rejoicing* by Huston Smith with Phil Cousineau. Novato, Calif.: New World Library, 2012. Used by permission.

Byrne, Erin. "Coltrane by Twilight," from *Images Between Pages*. Auburn, Wash.: Something Other Press, 2013. Reprinted by permission of the author.

McFerrin, Linda Watanabe. "A Little Night Music." First published in *San Francisco Chronicle Magazine*, as "Noche de los Muertos," October 12, 2003. Used by permission of the author.

Rumi, Mevlana. "You Have Opened a Secret Tonight." Previously unpublished translation No. 700; F-937 by Coleman Barks. Used by permission. © Coleman Barks.

Eliot, Jane Winslow. "Love at the Edge of the Grand Canyon," from *Soul Moments: Synchronicity*. Newburyport, Mass.: Conari Press 1997. Used by permission of Alexander Eliot.

Botsford, James. "Their 50th Anniversary," from *Them Apples*. Wausau, Wisc.: Sandyhouse Press, 2013. Used by permission of the author.

Shukman, Henry. "Night Feed," from *In Doctor No's Garden*. London: Jonathan Cape Ltd., 2002. Reprinted by kind permission of the author.

Part II: Nighthawks

Sappho. "Night Song, " from *Bittersweet Love: Poems of Sappho*, ibid. Used by kind permission of the translator.

Galilei, Galileo. "A Letter from Galileo." Unknown translator. www.columbia.edu/cu/tat/core/galileo.htm.

"The Night is Much More Alive," from *The Complete Letters of Vincent Van Gogh*. Edited by J. van Gogh-Bonger and V. W. van Gogh, and translated by J. van Gogh-Bonder and C. de Doot. London: Thames and Hudson, 1958.

Antler. "Campfire Talk," from *Selected Poems of Antler*. Berkeley: Soft Skull

Press, 2000. Used by kind permission of the author.

Carson, Rachel. "Alone with the Stars," from *Silent Spring*. First published in 1995. New York: Houghton Mifflin Company (Anniversary Edition), 2002.

George-Kanentiino, Douglas. "The Mohawk Thanks to the Stars." Original essay. Used by kind permission of the author.

Muir, John. "Glaciers by Starlight," from *The Wilderness World of John Muir*. New York: Houghton Mifflin Harcourt, 2001.

Byrd, Richard E. "Alone in the Arctic Night," from *Alone*. First published in 1938. Washington, D.C.: Island Press, 2003.

Hesse , Georgia. "A Night in an Igloo," from the forthcoming memoir *Slow-w-w Travel*. Used by kind permission of the author.

Eliot, Alexander. "Edward Hopper: The Nighthawk," from *The Timeless Myths*. New York: Plume Press, 1997. Used by kind permission of the author.

Molloy, Dara. "Bonfire Night on Inis Mór." Original essay. Used by kind permission of the author.

Harper, Tess. "Inis Mór Night." Original poem. Used by kind permission of the author.

Atwood, Margaret. "A Night in the Royal Ontario Museum," from *Animals in that Country*. Oxford University Press and Little, Brown, and Co.: 1968. This poem originally appeared in *The Atlantic Monthly*. Reprinted by permission of the author. © Margaret Atwood, 1968.

Byrne, Erin. "Café de Nuit," from *Images Between Pages*. Auburn, Wash.: Something Other Press, 2013. Used by kind permission of the author.

Balcomb, Stuart. "The Domain of Night: The Darkroom." Original essay. Used by kind permission of the author.

Beban, Richard. "Dear Air / Night Radio," poetry and song lyrics. Used by kind permission of the author.

Cable, Gudrun (Goody). "Reading at Night with My Father," from the forthcoming *Confessions of a Book-Loving Café-Owner and Hotelier*. Used by kind permission of the author.

Bakriges, Christopher. "Night Gigs in Motown." Original essay. Used by kind permission of the author.

Davis, Miles. "Miles of Country Roads," from *Miles* by Miles Davis, with Quincey Troupe. New York: Simon & Schuster, 1990. Reprinted with the permission of Simon & Schuster Publishing Group. Copyright © 1989 by Miles Davis. All rights reserved.

Morris, RB. "Amsterdam" (song lyrics), from the album *Spies, Lies, and Burning Eyes*, 2010. Used by permission of the songwriter.

Chadwick, Gregg. "Night Painting," from the forthcoming *The Speed of Light: Selected Art Essays*. Used by kind permission of the author.

Markham, Beryl. "West with the Night," from *West with the Night*. Eastford, CT.: Martino Fine Books, 2010.

Rosenblum, Mort. "The Moon over the Seine," from *The Secret Life of the Seine*. Boston: Da Capo Press, 2001. Used by permission of the author.

Li Po. "Drinking Alone by Moonlight," from *Translations from the Chinese*, by Arthur Waley. New York: Alfred A. Knopf, 1919.

Antler. "Bedrock Mortar Full Moon Illumination," from *Antler: The Selected Poems*. Berkeley: Soft Skull Press, 2000. Reprinted by permission of the author.

Kazantzakis, Nikos. "Zorba's Fire," translated and edited by Thanasis Maskaleris, from *The Terrestrial Gospel of Nikos Kazantzakis—Will the Humans Be Saviors of the Earth?* Ithaca, N.Y.: Zorba Press, 2011. Used by permission of Thanasis Maskaleris.

Hesse, Georgia. "Night Train," from the forthcoming memoir, *Slow-w-w Travel*. Used by kind permission of the author.

Haney, Bill. "Night Game," from the *Collected Works of Bill Haney*. Used by kind permission of the author.

Cousineau, Phil. "Pitch Dark," from *The Blue Museum: Poems*. San Francisco: Sisyphus Press, 2004. Used by permission of the author.

Clare, John. "Hares at Play," from *I Am: The Selected Poetry of John Clare*. New York: Farrar, Strauss, and Giroux Inc., 2003.

O'Connor, Flannery. "The Night Cry of the Peacock," excerpt from "The King of Birds" from *Mystery and Manners* by Flannery O'Connor, edited by Sally and Robert Fitzgerald. Copyright © 1969 by the Estate of Mary Flannery O'Connor. Reprinted by permission of Farrar, Straus and Giroux, LLC.

Morris, RB. "When Mockingbird First Heard Rock," from *The Mockingbird Poems*. Knoxville: Rich Mountain Press, 2013. Used by permission of the author.

Thoreau, Henry David. "Walking Walden," from *Walking*. San Francisco: Harper Collins, 1994.

Whitman, Walt. "Wandering at Night," from "The Sleepers" in *Collected Poems*. New York: Penguin Books, 1952.

Pratt, James Norwood. "San Francisco Nights," from *The Collected Poems* of *James Norwood Pratt*. San Francisco: North Beach Tea House Press, 2013. Used by kind permission of the author.

Aaland, Mikkel. "Elastic Midnight." Original essay. Used by kind permission of the author.

Cousineau, Phil. "The Night I Drove Kerouac Home," from *The Book of Roads*. Sisyphus Press, 2000. Used by permission of the author.

Rumi, Mevlana. "I Walk the City at Night." Previously unpublished translation No. 1266; F-71, by Coleman Barks. Used by permission. © Coleman Barks.

Iyer, Pico. "Night Walk in Manila." Originally published in *The New York Times Magazine*. Used by kind permission of the author.

Manguel, Alberto. "My Library at Night," from *The Library at Night*. New Haven: Yale University Press, 2009. Used by kind permission of the author.

Rumi, Mevlana. "Last Night, Alone." Previously unpublished translation No. 442; F-1035, by Coleman Barks. Used by permission. © Coleman Barks.

Part III: A Hard Day's Night

Abu Amir ibn al-Hammarah. "Insomnia," from *Poems of Arab Andalusia*. Translation © 1989 by Cola Franzen. San Francisco: City Lights Books. Used by permission of the publisher.

Zi Ye. "I Have Brought My Pillow" and "All Night I Could Not Sleep," from

Translations from the Chinese, ibid.

Yang-ti. "Winter Night," from *Translations from the Chinese,* ibid.

Ovid. "Untouched by Sleep," translated by Christopher Marlowe. Cited in *The Bed: Or the Clinophile's Vade Mecum,* by Cecil and Margery Gray. London & Redhill: Love & Malcomson Ltd., 1946.

Tate, Matthew. "The Fore Shift," by Matthew Tate, from *Allan's Illustrated Edition of Tyneside Songs.* Newcastle-upon-Tyne: Thomas & George Allan, 1866.

Poniewaz, Jeff. "Machines Shed Aluminum Tears," from *Selected Poems.* Milwaukee: Inland Ocean Books, 2013. Used by permission of the author.

Gandhi, Mahatma. "I Can See in the Midst of Darkness," from the compilation by M. K. Krishnan. Coimbatore, India: Vavaivan Press, n.d.

Chatwin, Bruce. "The Origins of Our Fear of the Dark," from *The Songlines.* New York: Penguin Books, 1981.

Cousineau, Phil. "Driving with Jack at Midnight," from *The Blue Museum: Poems,* ibid.

Morris, RB. "Take That Ride," song lyrics from the album *Take that Ride.* Knoxville: Oh Boy Records, 1997.

Weintraub, Stanley. "Silent Night in No Man's Land," from *Silent Night: The Story of the World War I Christmas Truce.* New York: Plume Books, 2002.

Tick, Edward. "Nhac Sanh," from the forthcoming *Poets Who Once Were Soldiers: Selected Poetry on War and Its Healing: 1984-2013.* Used by kind permission of the author.

Young, Gary. "In My Own House I Am a Stranger at Midnight," from *Cactus Spirituality—Pater Hilarion,* ibid. Used by kind permission of the author. © 2013.

LaChance, Rob. "The Dangers of Reading All Night," from *The Cabinet of Curiosities.* San Francisco: Sisyphus Press, 2010.

Chandler, Raymond. "The First Quiet Drink of the Evening," from *The Long Goodbye.* New York: Vintage Books, 1988.

McFerrin, Linda Watanabe. "Noche de los Muertos." Used by kind permission of the author. © 2013.

Emerson, Ralph Waldo. "Advancing on the Chaos and the Dark," from *Selected Essays by Emerson*. New York: Penguin Books, 2010.

Poniewaz, Jeff. "Burning the Midnight Oil," from *Selected Poems*. Milwaukee: Inland Ocean Books, 2013. Used by kind permission of the author.

Roethke, Theodore. "In a Dark Time." New York: Anchor Books, 1974. Used by permission of Anchor Books.

Thomas, Dylan. "Do Not Go Gentle Into That Good Night," from *The Poems of Dylan Thomas*. Reprinted by permission of New Directions Publishing Corp. ©1952 by Dylan Thomas.

Maclay, Sarah. "Bourbon," from *Whore*. Tampa, Fla.: University of Tampa Press, 2004. Used by kind permission of the author.

Jenkins, Joyce. "Childhood Radio Signal in the Alien Detroit Night," from *Joy Road*. Berkeley: Editions B.a.D., 2013. Used by permission of the author.

Manguel, Alberto. "Borges and the Darkness Visible," from *The Library at Night*. New Haven: Yale University Press, 2009. Used by kind permission of the author.

Morris, RB. "Night Train Home." Used by kind permission of the author.

Chadwick, Kent. "Tarde Noctem." Original poem. Used by kind permission of the author.

Dodgson, Charles Lutwidge (Lewis Carroll). "When Encountering a Ghost for the First Time," from *Bed-Time Stories: Entertainment for the Wakeful Hours*. Edgar Cuthwellis, ed. New York: Houghton Mifflin Co., 1979.

Joyce, James. "He Watched Her While She Slept," from "The Dead," in *Dubliners*. First published 1916. New York and London: Dover Publications, 1991.

Rumi, Mevlana. "The Night Will Pass," translated by Coleman Barks. Used by kind permission of Coleman Barks.

Sarton, May. "Lying Awake," from *Journal of a Solitude*. New York: W. W. Norton and Co., 1973.

"Tymnes," from *Cut These Words into My Stone: Ancient Greek Epitaphs*, translated by Michael Wolfe. Baltimore: Johns Hopkins University Press, 2013. Used by permission of the author.

Maclay, Sarah. "The Night Roses," from *The White Bride*. Tampa, Fla.: University of Tampa Press, 2008. Used by kind permission of the author.

LaChance, Rosemary. "Black Roses," from *Rosemary Means Remembrance*. San Francisco: Sisyphus Press, 2013. Used by kind permission of the author.

Part IV: The Dream Factory

Ono no Komachi. "I Fell Asleep," from *Women Poets of Japan*, Kenneth Rexroth and Ikuko Atsumi, eds. Translated by Kenneth Rexroth. New York: New Directions, 1977. Reprinted by permission of New Directions Publishing Corp. © 1977 by Kenneth Rexroth and Ikuko Atsumi.

Chang Tzu. "Chang Tzu's Dream (The Dream of the Butterfly)." Previously unpublished translation by Sat Hon with Alicia Fox. © Sat Hon 2013.

Po Chu-i. "A Dream of Mountaineering," from *A Hundred and Seventy Chinese Poems*, translated by Arthur Waley. New York: Alfred A. Knopf, 1919.

Pythagoras (attributed). "Let Not Sleep Come Upon Thine Eyes." Cited in *The Bed: Or the Clinophile's Vade Mecum*, ibid.

Leonardo da Vinci. "The Benefits of the Dark." Cited in *The Bed or the Clinophile's Vade Mecum*, ibid.

Dekker, Thomas. "Golden Slumbers." Cited in Oxford: *The Oxford Book of Quotations*, third edition, 1980.

Rumi, Mevlana. "Those Who Don't Feel This Love," translated by Coleman Barks and John Moyne. Used by permission of Coleman Barks.

Cousineau, Phil. "Windows and Doors," from *The Blue Museum: Poems,* ibid.

Anacreon (attributed). "The Midnight Guest." translated by Willis Barnstone. Used by kind permission of the translator.

Shakespeare, William. Sonnet 27. Various editions.

Coleridge, Samuel Taylor. "Dreaming of Kubla Khan," from the *Selected Poetry of Samuel Taylor Coleridge*. Various editions.

Poniewaz, Jeff. "Visiting My Brother One Summer Night After Rain," from *Selected Poems*. Milwaukee: Inland Ocean Books, 2013.

Olds, Sharon. "Looking at Them Asleep," from *Strike Sparks: Selected Poems: 1984-2002*. New York: Alfred A. Knopf, 2004. Used by permission of the publisher.

Maclay, Sarah. "Night Song," from *Whore*. ibid. Used by kind permission of the author.

De Quincey, Thomas. "Kant's Critique of Pure Sleep." Cited in *The Bed: Or the Clinophile's Vade Mecum*, ibid.

Poe, Edgar Allan. "A Dream within a Dream," by Edgar Allen Poe, from *A Collection of Poems by Edgar Allan Poe*. Grey Walls Press Ltd., 1948.

Stevenson, Robert Louis. "The Land of Nod," from *A Child's Garden of Verses*. Avenel Press by arrangement with Charles Scribner's Sons, 1948.

ud-Din Attar, Farid. "The Sentinel in Love," rendered into English by C.S. Nott from the French translations of Garcin de Tasst. From *The Conference of Birds*. Shambhala Publications Inc., 1971. ©1954 by C. S. Nott.

Botsford, James. "Postcard from the New Delhi Night," from *Them Apples*, ibid. Used by kind permission of James Botsford.

Shakespeare, William. Sonnet 43, from *The Poems: William Shakespeare*. New York: Bantam Classics, 1988.

Herrick, Robert. "The Vision to Electra," from *The Complete Poems of Robert Herrick*. Bloomsbury Publishing PLC, 1996.

Morris, RB. "Dreaming While I Drive," from *Early Fires*. Knoxville: Iris Press, 2007. Used by kind permission of the author.

Ficino, Marsilio. "A Renaissance Remedy for Sleeplessness," from *The Book of Life,* translated by Charles Boer. New York: Spring Publications Inc., 1982. ©1982 by Charles Boer.

Warfield, Joanne. "The Night of the Diaphanous Dream." Original essay. Used by kind permission of the author.

Steindl-Rast, Brother David. "Before Turning off the Lights," from "Encounter with God Through the Senses." Used by kind permission of the author.

Iyer, Pico. "The Mystery of Jet Lag," from "In the Realm of of Jet Lag," from *The Global Soul*. New York: Vintage Books, 2001. Used by kind permission of the author.

Burgess, Anthony. "Sleepwalking," from *Going to Bed*. New York: Abbeville Press, 1982. ©1982 by Anthony Burgess.

Part V: Morning Has Broken

Sappho. "Dawn" and "The End of a Party," from *Bittersweet Love: Poems of Sappho*, ibid. Used by kind permission of the translator.

Orpingalik. "An Eskimo Greeting to the Day," from *Eskimo Poems*, translated by Tom Lowenstein. Berkeley: University of California Press, 1992.

Li Po, "To Tan Ch'iu," from *Translations from the Chinese*, ibid.

Kobayashi Issa. "For Fleas, Also," from *The Penguin Book of Japanese Verse*, translated by Geoffrey Bownas and Anthony Thwaite. London: Penguin Books Ltd., 2009.

Basho, "The Night at Zensho-ji Temple" from *On a Narrow Road to a Far Province*, translated by Dorothy Britton. Revised edition. New York: Kodansha International, 1980.

Nepo, Mark. "The Throat of Dawn," from *Reduced by Joy*. Berkeley: Viva Editions, 2013. Used by permission of the publisher.

Beethoven, Ludwig van. "My Immortal Beloved," from *A Treasury of Letters*. Lincoln Schuster, ed. New York: Simon & Schuster, 1950.

Carroll, Lewis. "Alice Wonders: Was I Changed by the Night?" from *Alice's Adventures in Wonderland,* by Lewis Carroll. New York: Signet Classics, 2012.

Lalla. "It Gave Me Daring." Previously unpublished translation by Coleman Barks. Used by kind permission of Coleman Barks.

Khayyam, Omar. "Wake!" from *The Rubáiyát of Omar Khayyám*, translated by Edward Fitzgerald.

Gibran, Kahlil. "Speak to Us of Beauty," from *The Prophet*. Eastford, Conn.: Martino Fine Books, 2011.

Dekker, Thomas. "To Awaken Each Morning," from *The Non-Dramatic Works of Thomas Dekker*. London: British Library Historical Print Editions, 2011.

Pepys, Samuel. "Lying Single in Bed," Samuel Pepys, from *On Going to Bed*, ibid.

Ohiyesa (Charles Alexander Eastman). "Each Soul Must Meet the Morning Sun," from *Touch the Earth*, translated by T.C. McLuhan. New York: Abacus Books, 1988.

Young, Gary. "Waking in the Monastery," from *Cactus Spirituality—Pater Hilarion*, ibid. Used by kind permission of the author.

Klinkenborg, Verlyn. "Zero in the Dark," *New York Times*, January 6, 2013.

Thurman, Howard. "The Night View of the World," from *The Inward Journey*. ©1961 by The Howard Thurman Educational Trust, 220 Sacramento Street, San Francisco, Calif.

Rumi, Mevlana. "I Have Been Tricked." Translated by Coleman Barks. Used by kind permission of Coleman Barks.

Tick, Edward. "Delta Dawn," from the *Poets Who Once Were Soldiers: Selected Poetry On War and Its Healing: 1984-2013*, ibid. Used by kind permission of the author.

Lindbergh, Charles. "The Spirit of St. Louis in the Coming Dawn," from *The Spirit of St. Louis*. New York: Charles Scribner Sons,1953.

Shakespeare, William. "Our Little Life Is Rounded with a Sleep," from *The Tempest*. Various editions.

Iyer, Pico. "The Old City Before Dawn," from "In the Realm of Jet Lag," from *The Global Soul*. Used by kind permission of the author.

Barnstone, Willis. "White Nights," from *Stickball on 88th Street*. Pasadena, Calif.: Red Hen Press, 2010. Used by kind permission of the author.

Cousineau, Phil. "The Blind Watchmaker," by from *Night Train: New Poems*, published by Sisyphus Press, 2008. Used by permission.

A lengthy and comprehensive effort has been made to locate all copyright holders and to clear reprint permission rights. If any acknowledgements have been omitted, or any rights overlooked, it is unintentional. If the publisher is notified, any omissions will be rectified in future editions of the book.

INDEX
TO THE AUTHORS

● ◗ ○ ○ ○ ◖ ●

PHIL COUSINEAU is a freelance writer, filmmaker, photographer, art and literary tour leader, creativity consultant, flâneur, and nyctophiliac, a lifelong lover of the night. Cousineau has published over thirty books, which have been translated into numerous languages; earned twenty-five documentary film writing credits; and contributed to 50 other books. Cousineau has appeared frequently on NPR, CNN, and New Dimensions Radio, and appeared many times as a commentator on the mythic content of movies for Warner Brothers and Twentieth-Century Fox. His most recent books include *Wordcatcher*, which was named one of the Top Ten Books of the Year by NPR; *Beyond Forgiveness: Reflections on Atonement*, which won the *Science and Spirituality* Book of the Year, in 2012; and *Stoking the Creative Fires*, which won *Foreword* magazine's Gold Medal Award in 2008. Twice he has been nominated for Pushcart Prizes. He is a Fellow of the Joseph

Campbell Foundation and a Board Member of Sacred Sites International. Currently, he is the host and cowriter of the much-acclaimed television series "Global Spirit," which plays nationwide on PBS, and worldwide at www.globalspirittv.com. He lives with his family in the land of nighthawks, North Beach, San Francisco. For more information about Cousineau's books, films, lectures, workshops, writing consultations, and art and literary tours, visit www.philcousineau.net.

Phil Cousineau burning the midnight oil at the Zeitgeist Conference, in Phoenix, 2012.

Other books by the author

The Hero's Journey: Joseph Campbell on His Life and Work, 1990

Deadlines: A Rhapsody on a Theme of Famous Last Words, 1991

The Soul of the World: A Modern Book of Hours (with Eric Lawton), 1993

Riders on the Storm: My Life with Jim Morrison and the Doors, 1993 (by John Densmore with Phil Cousineau)

Soul: An Archaeology: Readings from Socrates to Ray Charles, 1994

Prayers At 3 A.M.: Poems for the Middle of the Night, 1995

UFOs: A Mythic Manual for the Millennium, 1995

Design Outlaws: Frontiers of the 21st Century (with Chris Zelov), 1996

Soul Moments: Marvelous Stories of Synchronicity, 1997

The Art of Pilgrimage: The Seeker's Guide to Making Travel Sacred, 1998

Riddle Me This: A World Treasury of Folk and Literary Puzzles, 1999

The Soul Aflame: A Modern Book of Hours (with Eric Lawton), 2000

The Book of Roads: Travel Stories from Michigan to Marrakesh, 2000

Once and Future Myths: The Power of Ancient Stories in Our Time, 2001

The Way Things Are: Conversations with Huston Smith, 2003

The Olympic Odyssey: Rekindling the Spirit of the Great Games, 2004

The Blue Museum: Poems, 2004

A Seat at the Table: The Struggle for American Indian Freedom, 2005

Angkor Wat: The Marvelous Enigma (photographs), 2006

Night Train: New Poems, 2007

The Jaguar People: An Amazonian Chronicle (photographs), 2007

Stoking the Creative Fires: 9 Ways to Rekindle Imagination, 2008

Around the World in Eighty Faces (photographs), 2008

Fungoes and Fastballs: Great Moments in Baseball Haiku, 2008

The Meaning of Tea (with Scott Hoyt), 2009

City 21: The Second Enlightenment (with Christopher Zelov), 2009

The Song of the Open Road (photographs), 2010

The Oldest Story in the World: A Mosaic of Meditations, 2009

Wordcatcher: One Man's Odyssey into the World of Words, 2010

Beyond Forgiveness: Reflections on Atonement, 2011

Shadowcatcher (photographs), 2012

The Painted Word: A Treasure Chest of Colorful Word Origins, 2012

And Live Rejoicing: Chapters in a Charmed Life (by Huston Smith with Phil Cousineau), 2012

The Soul and Spirit of Tea (with Scott Chamberlin Hoyt), 2013

Waiting for Kaline: A Baseball Fable for All Ages [forthcoming]

Who Stole the Arms of the Venus de Milo? [forthcoming]

Audio books

The Art of Pilgrimage, 1999
Once and Future Myths, 2002
The Way Things Are, 2004
Wordcatcher, 2010
The Painted Word, 2012

TO OUR READERS

Viva Editions publishes books that inform, enlighten, and entertain. We do our best to bring you, the reader, quality books that celebrate life, inspire the mind, revive the spirit, and enhance lives all around. Our authors are practical visionaries: people who offer deep wisdom in a hopeful and helpful manner. Viva was launched with an attitude of growth and we want to spread our joy and offer our support and advice where we can to help you live the Viva way: vivaciously!

We're grateful for all our readers and want to keep bringing you books for inspired living. We invite you to write to us with your comments and suggestions, and what you'd like to see more of. You can also sign up for our online newsletter to learn about new titles, author events, and special offers.

Viva Editions
2246 Sixth St.
Berkeley, CA 94710
www.vivaeditions.com
(800) 780-2279
Follow us on Twitter @vivaeditions
Friend/fan us on Facebook